When You Journeyed Homeward

Cynthia T. Kennedy

Eolus Press
Boulder, Colorado
2008

When You Journeyed Homeward
by Cynthia T. Kennedy
Copyright 2008. All Rights Reserved.

When You Journeyed Homeward

Library of Congress Control Number: 2008905207
ISBN: 978-0-9818117-0-3

1. Non-fiction, 2. Biographical, 3. Mountaineering

First Printing
Printed in the United States

Photography by Jerry Kennedy
Design by Sweet Success Press, Inc.

Produced and Distributed by

Eolus Press
P. O. Box 18941
Boulder ,Colorado 80308-1941
(303) 604-1600

When You Journeyed Homeward

Zebulon, Zebulon--
When you journeyed homeward,
How much of you returned?
What lay by your wife in the night?

Stephen Corey,
from "Tu Fu at Pikes Peak"

[1] From "Famous Mountains," in All These Lands You Call One Country (University of Missouri Press, 1992), © 1992 by Stephen Corey. Used by permission of the author.

When You Journeyed Homeward

Dedication

To Jerry
for teaching me to pace my climb

and to
Krishna, Sunita and Bishnu who will one day wonder what on earth led Jerry and me to each other and to Nepal, and who will find the answer, and many more answers, in the 'mountains'.

When You Journeyed Homeward

Table of Contents

When You Journeyed Homeward

PROLOGUE

Maurice Herzog once described the great climber, Raymond Lambert, as a man who found his "mode of self-expression in mountaineering." My husband, Jerry, is such a man. A climb is its own articulation, its own art form, and Jerry has little use for attempts at re-articulation of the experience. But I wish to tell the story, his and mine; therefore, you will find the words in this narrative to be mostly my composition. I make no apologies. It was necessary to find a single narrative voice to tell you this story; but the big climbs are Jerry's. Jerry's knowledge, experiences and opinions inform my own. He is the literal voice behind my voice in the mountain-climbing chapters, which I have constructed to a large degree based on his journals, photographs, and our years of conversation. To him I am grateful, not only for our shared years, but because it is he who lets the lawyer be the poet, and because he has graciously (and at times not so graciously) lived out his life quite literally in front of me and allowed me to share it here. I may ask the old question, what craziness leads a person up these monster peaks? But, having seen the hours put in on a manuscript such as this, Jerry believes it is *I* who must be questioned for sanity.

When You Journeyed Homeward

Hearth Fires

The great plinth of self-awareness is memory.

Stephen Tyman
from "A Fool's Phenomenology"

I had been waiting for the call from Kathmandu that would say the team was safely down. I didn't care if they had reached the summit of Cho Oyu. I never cared about summits. Jerry's voice quavered and had a question in it. "Cyndi?" As if to say, are you really there? And the next word told it all. Frostbite. His feet and hands were badly damaged. Too early to know how much could be saved. He'd had to walk out on damaged feet. He was lucky to be alive. Lucky.

It would be several days before he could get a flight out of Kathmandu. Then, with a lengthy layover in Bangkok, the journey home would be another thirty-six hours. The time would be agonizing for both of us, in very different ways.

"Where are you?" I asked hearing my own voice double back in the long-distance echo.

"Tibet Guest House," came the reply, then a pause, and his voice broke with restrained emotion, "The people here are just great."

This stutter, this hesitation, is a habit he has never lost. Whenever he speaks of anyone, or anything, Nepalese, he has a crack in his voice—an almost imperceptible waver. I've often conjectured that, when this happens, Jerry is letting loose the emotion of those difficult days—those days between coming off the mountain and returning home—in one-second bursts. Maybe one day he'll be free of the habit, though I doubt it. The years have given us so much more reason to choke up when speaking of Nepal. But, on that night, in that phone call—the call I would remember as having changed our lives—the constriction in the voice shocked me. Jerry is *not* the emotional type.

As we hung up, cutting that fragile electronic link between continents, I stood in the living room of our Boulder home like the fool in the first Tarot card, stepping blindly out over the cliff, like a sleeper on the precipice of waking, the horizon of my future a blur, my present a confusion of images made up of recollection of the past and fear of an unknown future. Nestling next to our two golden retrievers, Angel and B.J., lying on the 1960's blood red shag carpet that we had never replaced because, despite being tacky, it was still in good shape, I looked around our little home. The windows were closed against the brisk, early-October night and a fire crackled in the wood-burner

The furniture was what Jerry called "Early American College." The second-hand, pullout sofa hide-a-bed came from Jerry's college days. We'd reupholstered once, but the fabric was already worn again. Across from the couch stood the single antique—an over-sized rocking chair. Someone, sometime, had given it to Jerry, because of its size: Jerry is six-foot two. The lonely seat had echoed his absence now for two months.

The sickly green, limed-oak dining room table was his mother's from the 1930's, a ghastly piece, but the wood was solid oak and the chairs were the originals. The matching hutch was stored in the shed outside. We'd been meaning to have the whole set stripped, but the project had been on the "to do" list for over a decade. The remaining

The Maroon Bells, Pitkin County, Colorado.

furniture consisted of bookshelves—so cheap that the plywood shelves sagged despite the fact that the majority of the books were paperbacks.

I smiled to myself remembering a houseguest that had been sent our way by a friend. She looked at this room and said, "I don't understand. You are both lawyers and have furniture like this? A house like this?" We had made money and spent it on camping gear and on airline tickets. The walls were covered with memorabilia. Mostly there were photographs of mountains: A splendid shot down valley toward the Maroon Bells; Mt. Lindsey from Little Bear Peak; sunrise on Mt. Ranier—the sun a slit of Halloween orange between black rock and black sky; the one Jerry calls the "Oh my god, there *must be* a god shot" capturing a sun rising between two banks of clouds with just a narrow ridge of mountain at the bottom. A closer look at the "Oh my god" shot reveals footprints in the snow on the ridge, the only clue that the photographer is not in an airplane, but on the ground. At first the photograph appears to be in black and white, but the sunrise adds a purple tint to the shafts of light between the clouds, lending color. Jerry shot that one on Mt. McKinley—the mountain Jerry refuses to call McKinley, because the natives call it Denali. On the other wall hangs a picture of a climber on a steep snow ridge, a glacial valley curving below him like a twisting black highway. That was from Jerry's climb in the Pamirs in Kazikstan—the K Peak.

What would Cho Oyu add? I wondered. And at what cost? The trip to Tibet to climb Cho Oyu had cost thousands of dollars and had taken years to plan. But it was not financial cost that concerned me. Fear is the bile that turns an accepting mind to an anxious one, and I could taste acidity rising from the pit of my stomach. What now? Speculation would do no good. I could not turn my face to the future. I chose the past. The next few days were spent at my law office, clearing my calendar, getting as much work out of the way as I could, so that my time would be Jerry's when he finally arrived. In the evenings, I sat in the quiet of our home, with the two dogs, and tried to think back on how mountains had become so entangled in our lives.

I hear from those embattled in their pasts that memory is a walk through a mine field; however, it seems to me that memories, even cruel or irritating ones, are like yak dung, unpleasant only when fresh. When pressed into cakes and plastered on the garden wall to dry, they lose their rancor and, when cured, they provide the most welcome source of heat—at once fragrant and warming.

My memories would be my hearth fire until he came home.

A Mountain-Climbing

I am a wanderer and mountain-climber, said he to his heart....
And whatever may still overtake me as fate and experience—
a wandering will be therein, and a mountain-climbing:
in the end one experiences only oneself.

Friedrich Nietzsche
from "Thus Spoke Zarathustra"

Although I was born in Denver, Colorado, Queen City of the Plains, gateway to the Rocky Mountains, my first memories of mountains were the distant, jutting, snow-capped peaks of my mother's paintings. My father's mining career led him to a job with the Potash Company of America, in Canada. During the twenty-below-zero days of winter in Saskatoon, Saskatchewan, my mother painted in oils, from memory, her rickety easel placed strategically among the Lincoln logs and soldier camps of six snow-bound children. In contrast to the flat, colorless prairie in which we lived, the blue peaks of her paintings, capped in white, rose like promises, like fairy tales—places of respite and wonder, places far away.

I was eight the year my father decided he couldn't stand Saskatchewan another minute and loaded us in the station wagon for

Long's Peak, Allenspark, Colorado.

a summer trip. We drove 3000 miles from Canada down through Yellowstone and the Grand Tetons to the Colorado Rockies. Born and raised in a Ukrainian ghetto in Philadelphia, Dad had no experience with mountains until his high school science teacher who, finding him extraordinarily bright, told him stories of a place where smoke stacks didn't dominate the horizon, where beauty stuck her shoulders right out of the ground. That teacher recommended that my father study geology and apply to college, to the School of Mines in Golden, Colorado. He was accepted on scholarship and moved West to see his first mountains.

On that trip down from Canada, I saw them, too—the purple mountain majesties of song, huge and luring, reducing our car to a tiny insect as it twisted and turned its way through the Rocky Mountain roadways dotted at each treacherous turn with tiny white highway crosses. Not long after that summer trip from Saskatchewan we moved back to Denver. Both Dad and Mom had been Marines during World War II, and everything we did as a family was done with military efficiency; so, setting out on weekends and holidays, our family of eight went camping, fishing, and hiking. We could get that circus-size canvas tent up in twelve minutes flat with not a rock poking through. Those weekends were when the stuff of dreams turned to rock, the snow-capped peaks of paintings became glacier playgrounds, and the dabs of blue and green took on the smell of pine.

All was not idyllic. As we tumbled into the sixties, my father's workaholism turned to alcoholism, not an uncommon phenomenon for successful corporate men at the time—men who liked working in the mines but then found themselves in charge of divisions of engineers at international companies, sitting around conference rooms negotiating contracts, working seventy-hour weeks, traveling to distant places. I think of a Rodin sculpture, strong, compact, peasant-bodied men with strong hands used to pick-axes and shovels, straining out of the heavy base muck of mine tailings into the cold corporate air. The expression on their faces is one of clenched determination and confusion. Stuck in remote places managing mine construction for months at a time, with only each other and alcohol for company, they took to drinking heavily. At our home the strain was palpable, although there was only an occasional dramatic scene of Mother pouring booze down the drain and Dad slamming doors and driving off drunk. For the most part, my parents' inability to articulate or deal with the forces shaping their lives left us all embarrassed and nothing grew in that barren soil but silence—years of silence. "Please ask your father to pass the peas," my mother would say, seated at the same table as her husband. Eventually, Mother moved to a room downstairs, revived her interest in the spiritual (she had been a Rosicrucian in college), and took to meditating.

Meditation, like anything else, can be an addiction—a means of avoiding that which life has placed in front of you. My mother perfected that form of absenting herself. My own escape mechanism was mountains. The foothills of Colorado became a retreat, an escape, and a sanctuary from our troubled home. As one, and then another of us children could drive, we regularly headed for the mountains to hike or to just sit and watch the colored spray as it broke over the rocks of a mountain stream, convinced that if we could immerse ourselves sufficiently in the sound, the smell and the beauty of mountains, we would understand this mystery called life. Perhaps it was the lure of my mother's paintings. Perhaps she had painted mountains because it was true that mountains offered secret passage to the sublime. I was fifteen the year I came up with the theory of reverse evolution. Darwin was wrong, evolution was moving *away* from the clutter and chaos of complex entities, moving *toward* rock consciousness. After all, weren't the yogis all seeking some perfect calm; and what is so impenetrably calm, so perfectly unaffected by human emotion, as a mountain?

Eventually, I met someone to marry who also loved mountains—Jerry—but he didn't philosophize about them, he climbed them.

We met in law school at the University of Colorado. I had transferred from William & Mary in Virginia. I had hoped law school would be an opportunity to hone my intellect; but law school, with its calculated, cold academic environment and competition, was a sad disappointment. The state of Virginia itself did nothing to prevail on me to stay. A walk in the woods was almost impossible due to the undergrowth. I couldn't stand the spiders or the humidity, which seemed to slow both body and brain. How do I explain? The lack of precipitation, the alkalinity of the soil, the length of the days, that aspect of the American West that Wallace Stegner calls "aridity", and the texture of the light along the 40th Parallel combine to make the Rocky Mountains irresistible, to me anyway, which is perhaps nothing more than to say it is my home. After two years in Virginia, I was so disillusioned and homesick, I moved back. The University of Colorado accepted me. Now all I needed was a place to live.

I couldn't return to my parents' home. My father had finally confronted his alcoholism and was undergoing the twelve steps of Alcoholics Anonymous. But it was too late for the marriage. My mother and father had gotten divorced while I was in undergraduate school and my mother still lived in the house on the outskirts of Denver. It was a calm place now, filled with the tiny bonsai trees she had taken to cultivating—their miniature pine limbs twisted into position with malleable wires—as if the tiny trees of her paintings had turned corporeal in her home. But my mother's house was too far for a daily commute to Boulder, so Mom and I drove up, to Boulder, looking for a place for me to rent. After the graduate student "house" I had occupied in Virginia, squirreled into a cubbyhole of a room and sharing a shower with thirteen people, all I wanted in life was a place of my own. What had happened to rent prices in Boulder was shocking, and it was with a sinking heart that I decided to give the law school bulletin board a try. There was a handwritten note; "FIRST OR THIRD YEAR STUDENT WANTED TO RENT A ROOM." "Now there is a smart person," I thought. "He must be a second year student who doesn't want the competition in the sanctity of his home." William and Mary had taught me what competition was—law students stealing books to prevent others from getting the answers in the assigned library research tasks. I had endured the jealousy of the one friend I made when I wrote the best exam and got the "book award" in Constitutional Law. I did not like competition, and needed a room, so I called.

My mother and I found the modest brick home on Mohawk Street, just off Baseline, a mile and a half from the law school. Baseline runs precisely (or less than precisely actually, as it wends around lakes and land formations) along the 40th Parallel and was used as a "baseline" for surveying the American West. Following Baseline up, you arrive at Chautauqua Park, at the base of Flagstaff Mountain, with trails winding their way beneath, around, and eventually above the huge jutting slabs of rock they call the Flatirons. Follow the trails further and you find yourself high above Boulder on the top of Bear Peak, South Boulder Peak, Flagstaff, or Green Mountain. I knew those trails by heart.

It was with some trepidation that I returned to Boulder. I had left Boulder as an undergraduate seven years earlier after a suicide attempt. I would rather keep this part of the story to myself; but to be honest I must acknowledge how Flagstaff Mountain gave me back the life I thought I didn't want. I was nineteen at the time. Despairing of my own country's participation in a war I could not believe in—the Vietnam war, despairing at my own inability to intervene or make it better, of my own lack of understanding, confused and depressed by the failure of my parent's marriage and my father's alcoholism, unable to negotiate the terrain of college, lost in the crush of a campus of thirty thousand students all of whom seemed to have more direction and sense of self than I could muster, I hiked to my favorite pine tree in Chautauqua Park, high up on the meadow, just under the rock ledges. I had read that the American Indians had considered the suicide of a virgin to be a gift to the gods—giving oneself back to the godhead untouched, pure. Maybe there was some grace in the act. It was a warm October night, the harvest moon orange and full, just rising. I naively took the only weapon I had—a flimsy, double-edged razor blade—cutting across the wrist rather than up, encountering a tangle of tendons. Again and again I slashed, but then I stopped. Before me seemed to walk a parade of people, each of whom I recognized to *be me*: Orientals, men, some women, some children, some with green skin. The act of suicide was utter futility and did not rescue one. And then I was aware of the scent of dry pine needles, the warm breeze in my hair, and I wanted to be alive. I wrapped the hem of my long Indian print bedspread skirt around the bleeding wound and walked back down the mountain to the campus hospital. A doctor there with a quizzical look on his face sewed me up and gave me a tranquilizer. He knew what I was just learning: that life, whether it comes around once or a million times, is precious.

Since that time I have been convinced there are forces around us that are grounded in a deeper intelligence than we carry within our flimsy bodies. In times of great emergency they may make themselves felt, even seen, though never known. Their other intrusions in our lives are more subtle, though I am inclined to believe, no less calculated. Otherwise, there is no explanation but chance for my having met Jerry.

My mother and I stood awkwardly at the door for some time listening to the loud refrains of a Joe Walsh rock-and-roll tune pouring out the window, extolling the benefits of living in the Rocky Mountains. Eventually we found Jerry out back, up a ladder, painting the trim on the house green.

"You the one who called to see the room?" he asked, descending the ladder.

He was wearing nothing but jean cut-offs. Dark complexion, six-two, tan, healthy and grinning, at once a gaiety and yet a sorrow in the blue-green eyes. My mother mentioned this last as we drove off: "I wonder if he's been through a recent divorce."

"Well," he said later on the phone, "you can have the room if you help paint." So, a few days before classes were to start, I drove into Boulder with everything I owned (including my 1968 Martin D-25-00 guitar) in a Green 1968 Volkswagen Bug, and started painting the trim on the house.

"So, what's the name of the VW?" he asked.

"*Shean*. Green. Irish." I replied.

"Wrong political affiliation," he said, "Shean's a Protestant name. Gonna live in an Kennedy home, we'd better find a different name. Wolfgang. It's German, you know."

"It's green, it wants an Irish name."

"Okay, Paddy O'Wolfgang it is."

Then he led me through the house. Opening a closet, he said, "This is where we keep Derwood Kerby."

"Co-host of Candid Camera, right?" I asked, looking at the Kirby vacuum.

"And here in the kitchen is Wally the 1930's Chambers stove."

"Wally?"

"Wally Chambers. Baseball."

"You're out of my league naming things after sports," I quipped.

"Everything has a name," he replied. "You really don't know who Wally Chambers is? Jees, bet you never heard of Sherman Freightrain Loller, either. 1959 White Sox line-up, best ever. I had the full line-up in Baseball cards. My mother threw them away when I went to college. Can you imagine? I'm considering forgiving her, or suing her," he grinned, "That's why I'm going to law school."

A good quality in a man, I thought; takes care of things that are old, keeps them around, and even names them. I wondered if he'd keep a woman around as she aged.

I soon learned that Jerry was a very energetic fellow. Unlike the majority of law students, he not only worked, but worked full time, as a computer programmer. He managed to fit his classes around his work schedule, study at night, and still find the time to enjoy himself. Two weeks after I'd taken the room, I was lying on my bed when Jerry stuck his head in and said, "You want to go to a party in the mountains? I've got a free ticket."

I looked down at the administrative law book I was reading, and the decision was an easy one. We jumped into Jerry's 1968 Chevy Impala, Florence, and headed for the Beer & Steer, an annual extravaganza put on by the Homebrewers' Association at the Heil Ranch up Left Hand Canyon, on twenty acres of land. At one end of the meadow was the beer: kegs and kegs and kegs of competing home brews. A pig had been cooking in an underground pit since four that morning and was just being served as we arrived. The entry fee was a dish to share, so there were dozens of tables covered with an astounding array of foodstuffs: watermelons, casseroles, pickles and pies, salads and salsas. For those who wanted bratwurst or steak or chicken or fried tofu, there were grills with coals lighted.

At the other end of the meadow a bluegrass band was performing, the sweet fiddle music mixing with the tinny banjo and the regular strum of the guitar in a combination as complex, spicy, and smooth as a good barbecue sauce. The sun's intensity was filtered by stands of aspens, their coinlike leaves shimmering gold. Jerry led me through the crowd to a group of his friends sitting on a blanket.

"You must be the new roomie." The voice came from a round-faced fellow with a shaggy mustache and longish hair. "I'm Michael. This is Dave," he said, "We work with Jerry at Graftek. Settle in." They handed me a glass of mead, a champagne-like honey brew, and I sat, leaned back against a tree, and closed my eyes, enjoying the music accompanied by the energetic discussions of Jerry and his friends as they debated software solutions, politics, home brew and hops. Their talk was so full of laughter, so extroverted, so socially engaged. I had made it down the mountain that undergraduate moonlit suicide attempt night so many years ago, but I'd never learned to make friends or feel comfortable in company. School had been a loner enterprise for the most part. I envied those who had more social aspects to their lives and was touched by how willing these friends of Jerry's seemed to be to include me.

Late in the afternoon, a woman stopped by—a tall, blond, lanky, good-looking creature in tight jeans and a halter-top. The conversation stopped. Nobody invited her to sit as they courteously said, "Hello, Claire."

"This must be the new roommate," she said, scrutinizing me without embarrassment.

"Cyndi\Claire" said Jerry, but his voice was flat. He got up and walked off with the woman, keeping his distance from her.

Michael, the mustached, waited until they were out of earshot and leaned to me to say, "They lived together for like five years, broke up over a year ago, but she still plays with his head."

Perhaps that explained the sadness my mother had guessed was a

B. J. Hunnibear and Angel.

divorce. Michael continued, "She read some funky, feminist literature, decided relationships are the pits. Her solution was to liberate herself, which, translated, meant sleeping with any one of Jerry's friends that would indulge her."

"She's nice looking," I said, straining to see the two figures moving through the crowd and into the trees. Jerry still was not touching her. I didn't want him to and the thought made me blush. I was twenty-seven years old and had sworn off men—the only date I'd had in three years was with my guitar. I had one year of law school left and already had an appointment as a clerk to a federal judge upon graduation. I even had an offer in hand for a job after that, with a 17th Street law firm in Denver. I did not need an emotional entanglement, particularly with someone otherwise involved.

"It led to a significant attrition of friends." Michael was laughing. He jumped to his feet and offered to bring us all another beer.

Across the meadow, Jerry and Claire moved into the shelter of the trees. It wasn't but a few minutes later that he returned. He did not bother to sit down. "Let's go," he said to me.

I gathered my things: purse, the novel I had not cracked, my sweater, and this new thing, this breach of my promise to myself not to get involved with a man.

Jerry didn't open the car door for me, and we sat in silence as the big Chevy rattled over the winding dirt roads at a dangerous pace. He turned on the headlights as the thin light of day's end strobed through the trees and then turned dark.

"She's pretty," I finally said. I could feel him tense.

"It's over," he replied.

"I'm not," I said. The silence that followed was so complete I wasn't sure for a moment that I'd actually said the words. But he must have heard. The car slowed, purred more rhythmically, then stopped where the dirt road ended and we were to turn onto the highway that would take us back to Boulder.

Then he made a motion with his head as if to say simply "Come." Quivering in the way of a woman not touched in years and about to be touched, I slid over the silken seat to his side. He took my head into both his large strong hands, pulling back my hair, and kissed me deeply.

Within another week, I had written him a song of his own:

There's a history of highways in your eyes.
We've met before, or maybe no,
It's just a certain sorrow that I recognize...

I watched him curiously at first. I'd never known anyone so confident, in everything he did. His academic credentials were impressive and included an undergraduate degree in general engineering from the University of Illinois and a masters in computer programming from Illinois Institute of Technology. He was in his second year working toward a law degree from the University of Colorado. Yet he was so physical—skiing, climbing—and had stories of growing up Catholic, of moving around a lot, of putting himself through college driving truck. Jerry never had difficulty striking up a conversation with anyone, and never, ever put himself above anyone because of his education. He could discuss economics or politics but was just as passionate about the White Sox, beer, and Chevy Impalas dated 1968. He was connected to life in a way I wasn't. Despite my academic successes, I had not overcome my tendency to view the world as an alien and hostile place or the habit of seeking refuge in my room in the quiet solace of my own depressions. But Jerry had ways of luring even me

B. J. Hunnibear and Angel.

out of my cave.

"Well," he said, a few days before Thanksgiving, "since there are two of us to keep an eye on it, what would you think of a puppy?" The first golden retriever was B.J. Hunnibear. Then, a week or two before Christmas, a fellow Jerry worked with called to say he'd heard Jerry was looking for a dog, and he had just gotten a golden puppy a few days earlier but couldn't keep it. Could he bring it over? Jerry wasn't home and already had a puppy, but I said yes.

She was the tiniest little thing. Around her neck was tied a tiny red ribbon. Jerry had spent weeks choosing his own puppy for good breeding, and this little one was clearly the runt of some litter and no show dog. I was afraid he'd say, "One dog's enough," but I underestimated the generosity of his big Irish heart. He walked in, took one look, grinned and said, "Sure."

Jerry insisted dogs be named after mountains. The first pup was officially named for Osito de Sangre de Cristo (Little Bear of the Sangre de Cristos—Blood of Christ Mountains) a peak in Southern Colorado. It was B.J. for short (Bear Junior after Jerry's last dog, Bear, an Irish Setter). I wanted to name the new puppy Angel, for Christmas; so, we settled on Angel of Shavano—Shavano being a 14,000' peak with a snowfield called the Angel (the angel weeps in spring it is said, to irrigate the farmers' fields below).

Thirsty Boots

Take off your thirsty boots and stay for a while/
Your feet are hot and weary from a dusty, dusty mile.

Eric Anderson
from "Thirsty Boots"

I met Jerry at the airport and almost didn't recognize him. He was thin and gaunt, having lost thirty pounds, and he was sporting a half-gray, scraggly beard. His eyes were dulled by pain. I reached to touch him and he recoiled, pulling in the fingers crusted with black. He said dully, "Let's get out of here," shouldered his backpack, and moved ahead of me.

We didn't say much on the drive. After ten years of marriage we knew how to be silent together, but this was not the comfortable, relaxed, shared silence of husband and wife; it was a colder, clenched, frightened thing. I reached to turn on the radio, anything to fill the vacuum of sound; but as soon as the static crackled into music, he reached to turn it off. I restrained myself from making some snotty remark about how his choice was somehow more important than mine. That was how I usually defended myself when our wills clashed on matters small or large, letting the lawyer in me advocate for her position. But for once I couldn't read him. I didn't know what was at stake. I let it go.

John the Bootmaker.

When we got home he took off his boots—the leather boots hand-made by John Caulden—boots that had seen their way up mountains in Alaska, in the Pamirs, and now Tibet. They looked old, thirsty. As Jerry removed the thick wool socks, I had to keep myself from reacting. He had said he might lose some toes, but the feet were dark gray, top and bottom, far past the metatarsal head—the place where the toes join the foot. Didn't he know? But perhaps I didn't know, and it was superficial. So I said nothing.

That night, as he lay in bed, I leaned over to touch my husband. He jerked away and I withdrew, shaken.

Angel and B.J., now eleven, sniffed curiously at Jerry's feet, and at the piles of tents and duffels littering the house, filled with scents that must seem to the hounds as exotic as the words sounded to me—Tibet, Nepal— but the dogs were as reserved as I in their greeting, and Angel, who had grown accustomed during Jerry's lengthy absence to sleeping with me on the bed, chose the floor. It wasn't the time to tell Jerry that B.J. had been throwing up lately, chronically. It wasn't the time.

The next morning, as we were leaving for the doctor's office, Jerry dug into his pack and handed me a silver ring with a turquoise stone.

"I got this from my favorite Tibetan yak herder," he said. "It's probably not real silver, but he was an interesting fellow. Spoke very good English. Wanted to study to be a dentist and I take it had been out of Tibet studying. He helped us on the way up, but wasn't there on the way down. I ran into him in the village of Tingri, and he said the Chinese had found out he was speaking English to the Americans and had spent the time we were on the mountain in jail for it. So I gave him fifty bucks. He gave me the ring."

"Turquoise is supposed to be a healing stone," I said hopefully, slipping the delicate thing on my finger, and we left to meet our appointment.

The look on the doctor's face as Jerry's socks were removed confirmed my fears. He was going to lose all the toes, some unknown portion of the feet, the tips of fingers. Jerry was lying on the doctor's table, and the doctor spoke, directing his comments to us both, explaining that with frostbite one does nothing for forty-five days, letting the body show by demarcation – the blackening of the skin – where to cut. I watched Jerry's face. There was only a slight flinching of the muscles, but then the expression froze into a hardened mask of determination. He said nothing, but I could see he was trying desperately to overcome the vertigo, the sense of falling, the knowledge that there was no rope to arrest his fall. I wasn't the only one who sensed the depth of the reaction. The doctor ordered that Jerry be taken to the hospital for sedation.

"Get me out of here," Jerry demanded less than an hour later. His voice was controlled, but determined. I looked over at him and gasped. He was ripping the I.V. tube out of his arm.

"Jerry, you can't do that…"

He tossed his head toward the pole. "It's a goddamned sulfate antibiotic, Cyndi. You know I'm allergic to sulfates." Despite piles of forms and orange stickers on the file stating that Jerry had allergies, the nurse had hooked him up to receive a drug to which he is completely allergic. A few moments later and Jerry quite likely would have been dead or in anaphylaxis fit. Life, for each of us, hangs on each I.V. pole, waits at each intersection. One should proceed with caution and gratitude.

While getting the I.V. confusion resolved, it became apparent this hospital was no place for Jerry. The buzzers and intercoms, the shuffling of nurses and the clatter of beds and meal-carts, let us know a stay would not be restful. It would be the first of many hospital stays, and not the last disappointment. I spoke to the doctor. Surely being at home would be more conducive to healing? The doctor agreed and released Jerry after giving him a shot of morphine. I was pulling the car into the driveway before it dawned on me that a 5'4" woman was not going to be able to get a 6'2" man under the influence of narcotics, out of the car, up the steps and into the house. What was the doctor thinking? So, I left Jerry in the car while I called a neighbor who graciously appeared to help me drag Jerry into our home.

In contrast to the noise of the hospital, home felt like a sanctuary. Jerry slept and I worried. What would be his capacity? Would the hands recover or parts be lost? Would he walk? I hesitated to hope because, in times of stress one has a tendency to try to make deals with god, whether one believes in any particular god or not. Leave his hands and I'll give you his feet. Leave his feet and I'll give you…. My god, his feet were so important to him, had carried him up so many mountains. Which was more important? There had been a time in his life when he had not climbed, surely, but I had not known him then.

Before we met, Jerry had already taken on the challenge of climbing all the peaks over fourteen thousand feet in Colorado. There are fifty-four of them. There were fifty-three when he started, but the geographical survey teams of the United States keep measuring things and the lists change. He didn't care. The goal was not to finish but to explore Colorado, to journey through valleys and high deserts, to explore every aspect of the worlds mountains create: glaciers, moraine, tundra.

At first the situation was awkward: he'd leave for weekends to climb with friends, and I would stay home with the dogs and my guitar feeling abandoned. Finally I asked him, "Why can't I come?"

"Everyone needs to be responsible for himself in the mountains," he said. "You can come if you take the CMC course first."

'CMC' meant the Colorado Mountain Club, which offered a comprehensive mountain climbing course every spring. So, after returning from a day as a lawyer in Denver, I'd rush to attend lectures on ice climbing and avalanche rescue. I was the only one in a suit. On weekends, Jerry slept in while I rose at 5:30 a.m. to trudge miles up the canyons around Boulder with a half a dozen other neophytes, carrying heavy Goldline rope to climb miscellaneous outcroppings.

The author and B. J. Hunnibear on Mt. Democrat
(14,148 feet), Park County, Colorado.

One day, having spent the night in a tent with a woman obsessed by her make-up, climbing up the glacier to attend my first ice-axe-on-snow lesson, I found myself actually grateful that Jerry had given me crampons and not perfume for Valentine's day. I graduated the CMC course feeling only slightly less proud than when I accepted my law degree.

After that, on weekends, in sleet and sun, snow and pelting ice, sometimes on snowshoes, skis, or crampons, with heavy pack and ice axe, I diligently plodded up peaks behind Jerry, the two golden retrievers running circles around us and pulling alerts on the ptarmigan, marmot, and pica.

I cried on the first fifteen peaks we climbed together. They were grueling days. Unused to the need to pace myself, I wanted to stop often for breath. Jerry's motto was "slow down, but don't stop." His expectations left me feeling inadequate to the job, and when his pace exceeded mine I was left huffing my way up steep alpine meadows on my own, my feet tangling in the course undergrowth of pathless routes. Inevitably, I would collapse emotionally at about 13,500 feet, where the nausea started to rise and my breath failed due to the altitude. Jerry would be on the summit by that time and the dogs never felt loyal enough to stay with the one lagging behind.

I remembered once when my father, Paul, took me down into a mine he was in charge of building. One of the foremen came up to me and said, in a thick Irish accent, "Your dad's a demanding fellow. Bet you never got any pocket money out of that one." And now I wondered why I had chosen a man to marry who was as demanding in his expectations as my own father had been. Even Jerry once said, "You don't work with Paul, you work for him." Well, you don't climb with Jerry. You are welcome to come along, but he won't haul your weight and doesn't expect you to haul his. So, if Dad was a Rodin sculpture, Jerry was a Henry Moore—a similarly dark, formidable, solid presence, but more abstract, smoother, harder to grasp.

Early the next morning, the telephone rang. The Cho Oyu team gear was sitting down in Denver in customs.

"Can't the other team members deal with it?" I asked Jerry.

"No," came the reply, "Dick's in Greeley. The others are sight-seeing in Thailand." His voice was curt, short with disdain, thick with the painkillers the doctor had given him. Greeley was only an hour away. It seemed odd to me that the others hadn't come home, hadn't called. Did the other climbers know how badly Jerry was damaged?

I drove with this bandaged man lying in the back of the station wagon, propped up by pillows, hands and feet wrapped in gauze. The customs man took one look at Jerry and decided not to even examine the bags. Anyone who had suffered so badly, even if they had smuggled something in from Nepal, were welcomed to their plunder.

When we got home, I unpacked, sorted gear and brushed out tents. In one of the duffels I found a battered steno pad—Jerry's diary of the climb—along with the tape of my songs I'd sent with him to Cho Oyu, and the two small, green tourmaline stones that he had carried. They were to be set in rings for our tenth anniversary.

Tenth anniversary. There was some discussion as to the arrangements for the wedding. Jerry was raised Catholic but, the way he tells it, from the day he bit the nun in first grade and got the appropriate corporeal punishment, organized religion did not sit well with him. He was twelve and delivering newspapers when he saw Cardinal John Cody getting into a brand new Lincoln Continental.

The obese man was helped into the back by his chauffeur. Jerry's thoughts turned to how his mother had gone back to work while raising five children in order to make ends meet, and of how they were still supposed to tithe ten percent of the family's income to the church. How could this obscenely fat man afford to gorge himself on their money? Jerry could read the license plate as the Cardinal drove away. It said, "No. 1." Religion equated to hypocrisy after that.

Years later, as his parents' marriage failed—the fragile threads of a 1940's war marriage proving too infirm to span the gap of changing times—Jerry was horrified that the Catholic Church, in order to allow his father to remarry, annulled the first marriage. In Catholic nomenclature, that rendered five children bastards and a marriage of twenty-five years nonexistent. Jerry understood this state of affairs had been procured by a donation. It did nothing to endear Jerry to the church, and he adamantly refused a church wedding. Nor would he invite his parents, which would mean forcing his mother to encounter his father's current wife.

My parents were also divorced and my father remarried, but both my parents lived in Colorado and my mother said she could handle meeting my father's wife, though it would be their first encounter. Dad had recovered after his bout with alcoholism (I think of the Rodin character freeing itself from the mud and standing, liberated) and through his recovery and Alcoholics Anonymous, he had become a minister.

"So, what do you say? If my dad does the ceremony, it's one less person we have to invite; but, of course, I'd have to have my mom too, to be fair." I'd made my case.

"Okay," said Jerry, "as long as we keep it under ten people and I get to wear blue jeans."

I shared Jerry's cynicism for organized religion; so, we agreed to be married in the 'church of the mountains' and chose the top of Flagstaff Mountain in September. It has the advantage of a road to the top and a small amphitheater. We rented it for the morning for $15.00 from the City of Boulder, and went to the 1981 Beer and Steer for our reception. We'd known each other almost exactly one year.

That was ten years ago. Now the task was to go to the laundromat to wash duffels and haul sacks. Our ancient washer (Charybdis) and dryer (Scylla) could not handle the bulky items. As the front-loading coin operated washers went round, my questions went round. Would Jerry survive this? When would he let me know what had happened? What had happened? Where were the other climbers while I was washing the group duffels and tents? Did they know the extent of Jerry's damage? Why in god's name didn't they carry him out on a litter or something? I had read Tichy's account of the climb in 1954—the first successful ascent of Cho Oyu. The man's hands had been badly frostbitten. The book contains a picture of the injured man being carried in a litter. Why not Jerry? My questions began to knot around a core, like a sheet in the dryer that catches a hand towel in its center and winds itself into a rope. I didn't recognize what was caught in the core as anger; but it was. How could the climbers be seeing the tourist sights in Thailand while we waited for the gangrene to mark the line of amputation? I did recognize another emotion stirring within me. I was beginning to feel sorry for myself. Self-pity, Jerry himself had taught me, is not acceptable.

One weekend Jerry had talked me into climbing Mt. Lincoln, a fourteener, in mid May. The climb up was long and grueling. Road closures due to snow added several miles, and the snow on the route was deep. We never reached the summit of Lincoln because the day was getting short. We settled for 14,200-foot Mt. Cameron—only a couple of hundred feet from the summit of Lincoln, but considered a sub-peak because of its proximity to the higher peak. The hike out was absolute misery. As we post-holed through snow up to our waists, our snowshoes just sank. Finally, neither of us could raise our feet; the weight of the snow on the surface of the sinking snowshoes was too much. We ended up trying to keep our weight more evenly spread by taking off the snowshoes and lying across the snow, literally swimming out.

We piled into the car for the two-and-a-half-hour trip home. It was on that trip, with a spasming cramp in my right leg, that I gave up feeling sorry for myself. Like lichen, which does not exist without both its components, alga and fungus, self-pity is a symbiotic species; it does not thrive without a sympathizer, an audience, and I could see that in my husband I would never find such an audience. Not only had Jerry lured me out of my cave of solitude, but out of self-pity as well.

Out of self-pity and into adventure. There was risk. One Spring, after sleeping in a tent on snow, we climbed Kit Carson from the southern route, up a steep glacier. The morning had been unpleasant in the extreme, because another group behind us also attempting the peak, led by a loud woman wearing plastic boots (overdress for this glacier, where leather boots and crampons were fine) and a halter-top (underdress for this circumstance where sun on snow can blind you and burn your skin to a crisp in a dozen minutes). If the mountains were our church, silence was our creed, and there was no blasphemy more egregious than that of polluting a perfect day with unnecessary banter. Sound expands in a mountain cirque, echoing off the valley walls, and Jerry and I winced every time the woman's Texan drawl bounded off the rocks.

The woman eventually left her group behind, still communicating with them by yelling, and I was feeling particularly unfit as she passed us at a quick clip. I felt better an hour or so later when I was still going at my steady pace and we had left her 1,000 feet below us. As the distance increased to 2,000 feet, we could no longer hear her whine. She had turned around.

At the crest of the glacial coulior, the route traversed along a rocky ridge to the summit. Dark clouds began to pour over the ridge, and the air became quiet and gloomy. Jerry was already on the summit, and as I scurried along the thin ledge in his direction, I stopped, mesmerized by a high tone, like a single note on a violin. "Listen Jerry," I said, "the rocks are singing." Just as I spoke, the ice axe in my hand started vibrating and giving off a high whistle, "And my ice…" I began, but he was yelling, "Get the hell off the ridge." Even at 14,000 feet the brain is slow. I had read about electricity. I had read about the rocks singing, but when the Sirens sang to me, I was captivated and stood motionless, unaware of the danger. My body vibrated with the magic of the ringing music in my blood. Jerry moved toward me, trying to break the spell. I heard his shout as something distant, unalarming. As he drew close enough, he physically shook me. The look on his face, a look of concern, of danger, jolted me out of my mesmeric trance. With hair and nails vibrating, I followed Jerry down under a ledge where we huddled, holding each other and listening to the cracks of lightning above us.

Over time, I learned to pace myself and no longer resented the solitude of the climbs. Even when two climb together, tied by ropes, there is a separateness about the endeavor. Climbing doesn't leave a lot of breath for conversation. Sometimes we didn't talk at all—six hours, sometimes eight, sometimes sixteen.

There are those who say that our experience of nature is linguistic, that because we are given to language the very nature of that tendency supersedes and overshadows all other aspects of experience, so colors activity, encounter and emotion that all human activity or thought is of the domain of that language, and that, therefore, the encounter with nature is linguistic. I don't agree. Following Jerry up mountain after

B. J. Hunnibear on Elbert Peak (13,800 feet) watching Mountain goats from across the valley.

mountain, I—one who loves reading and writing—came to be grateful at the opportunity to leave my linguistic tendencies behind; I came to understand that one's relationship to nature is the one aspect of being human that transcends barriers of time, of language, that joins rather than separates us from the other species and the elements of the natural world. The language of the mountains speaks to us in the blood, so to speak. Mountains were no longer a philosophy, though it wouldn't be too far off track to say they were a religion.

Not all persons who chance upon mountains are snagged by them the way we were. I know a dozen Denverites who just never happen to "get to the mountains," who stare at the purple majesties through some of the world's worst brown smog and are not perturbed. A recent statement from a Boulder city council person referred to the Flatirons— those great heaving masses of crimson rock jutting from the sides of the mountains circumferencing the town—as the "mountain backdrop." Just a scrim against which the drama of their lives is acted out. To us they were no backdrop; they were the root of our relationship.

Climbing changed us both: inadvertently, by a demanding schedule of fitness and climbing, Jerry had pulled me from the depths of my melancholia. He simply ignored my depressions and, expecting I would have the good sense to ignore them too, finally imbued me with the strength to abandon them. Maybe I didn't need to engage in such tortuous introspection. The very stasis of the relationship offered balance. I didn't analyze it. I just spent less time in my room, in my books. We had become best friends and climbing companions. The marriage was rock-firm. By the time Jerry finished the fourteeners, I was as addicted as he was and we started on those peaks over 13,000 feet. Jerry took photographs. In one B.J. Hunnibear, the male golden, by then a full-chested, regal dog with a lion's mane, stands at an altitude of perhaps 13,800 feet on Elbert Peak. He has an alert, attentive thrust to his head, his nose taking the wind. Joining that photo with two others, gives a panoramic view of the continental divide, the red rock ridge, just a film of snow on the crests of the peaks, and, to the right, two small dots on a rock ledge across the valley. A fourth picture,

B. J. Hunnibear's mountain goats.

Left: The Diamond on Long's Peak, Allenspark,

shot with a telephoto lens, reveals the subject of Mr. Hound's attention—two burly mountain goats making their way over the ridge, standing proud among the huge, granite blocks.

While my memories had taken me up half the mountains in Colorado, I'd successfully washed and partially dried seven duffels and three tents. I loaded the gear in the car and drove home. Activity helped. It was harder to walk back into the house.

Death Gestures

Death is our eternal companion," don Juan said....
"An immense amount of pettiness is dropped
if your death makes a gesture to you,
or if you catch a glimpse of it...

Carlos Castaneda
from "Journey to Ixtlan"

Jerry sat in the big rocker with his feet up on a footstool, wrapped in bandages. The silly old ninety-pound Mr. Hound was on his lap. I laughed, but Jerry didn't.

"What is wrong with B.J.?" he said, his voice accusatory. "He's thrown up twice while you were gone. He's lost a lot of weight."

Just after Jerry left for Cho Oyu, our friends Chris and John had called and invited me camping and to climb a 14'r. They'd chosen Shavano and I wanted Angel, the girl hound, to climb the peak after which she had been named, so I said yes. Jerry had climbed it years before.

It was a beautiful fall trip and I have a photo of myself on the summit of Shavano with the two dogs. Looking back, you can already see the

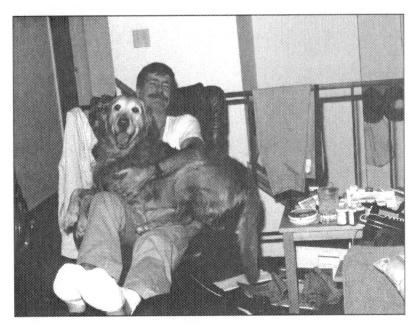

Jerry with B. J., our 90 pound lap dog.

white in B.J.'s face, sort of like a nowhere man mask, and his silly grin. It was on that trip that B.J. started to throw up. Once, twice in the night, soon a dozen times. I'd had him not only to the veterinarian in town, but to the specialists in Ft. Collins, a university renowned for its veterinary school. Doctors. Tests. No tumors, no cure. The dog was losing weight. I nursed him. I made special small meat pellets of raw hamburger and rice and fed them to him individually. He slept on a raised board slanted to help the food stay down. I read books on holistic animal medicine. The vet complimented me on how long I was managing to keep him alive.

"It's megasophagus," I informed Jerry, "an inability of the esophagus to get food to the stomach. Our esophagi are smooth muscle, dogs are striated, and they wear out. He can't get the food from the mouth to the stomach." And then I started to cry. "He's starving to death."

Jerry's face went even grayer, for a moment only, then his hand started rubbing the dog's ears and he said in a soothing, friendly voice, a voice I recognized by tone because it was the one I was trying so often to maintain myself, those days, falsely optimistic, "Hey, big guy, how you doing, huh? Miss me?"

I hid my own feelings and busied myself cleaning the carpet, but I was thinking of death. I did not have much experience with death, and I didn't know that Jerry had more experience than I until he confided in me one Sunday not long after we were married.

Behind our home loomed Green Mountain. The hike up takes an hour and a half. Along the way there are several resting spots from which one can look out on Boulder, following the green tendril of Bear Creek as it meanders down. Bear Creek ran behind our house, so we could easily pick out our roof, right where the creek intersected Mohawk Street. On this particular day, Jerry and I sat on the rocks trying to pinpoint his place of employment. After law school he'd decided to stay in software development. The pay was much better than entry-level law positions, the job was close to home, and Jerry enjoyed the work. There it was—Graftek. My own position as a first year associate for a law firm in Denver, kept me commuting two hours a day and putting in long hours. The silence and respite of our Sunday hikes became all the more important.

We gazed out at our little world. We were married, and it was time to ask the question. "What about kids?" I said.

"No," he said decisively, "When I was born, I had a small tumor at the base of my brain stem. They operated and it was nothing to be concerned about. It was nothing but hair. A couple of years later, my sister Sue was born with a similar tumor. Because mine was nothing, they didn't operate immediately. They should have. Hers was water and she had to go through numerous surgeries for what they call 'water

Longs Peak at full noon, July 1987.

on the brain,' leaving her motor function and speech impaired. The surgeries left scar tissue that caused epileptic seizures. She was handicapped at a time when it wasn't accommodated. In fact, she was shunned."

"You've never even mentioned her." I was shocked at the ability of this taciturn man, to whom I had made a lifetime commitment, to keep things so deep inside; but it explained his independence. The little boy whose mother had to work to pay the medical bills and whose attention was always on the needy one. He simply took control of his own life at an early age and didn't look back.

"She died the summer you came, about two months before we met. An overdose of Phenobarbital; she was twenty-eight. The family position is that it was an accident."

Finally I understood the sorrow in those green Irish eyes. It wasn't just the woman, Claire. The sadness had been intense when we first met, a palpable weightiness, but had eased over time. Still, it lingered in his eyes.

"So, I'm afraid of the genetics," he said. "No kids."

He had lost a sister. As with most things, my familiarity with Shakespeare's "grim ferryman" was conceptual, not real:

Several years after we were married, in early June, I cannot even remember the year, Jerry and I were camping above Ouray, Colorado, below Mt. Sneffels. After a good long day of hiking across crusty snowfields we were stopped by a cornice just short of the peak. It was too unstable to cross and we retreated, returning to camp wet and exhausted. A meal of chili was followed by a mushroom or two – psilocybin mushrooms. I'd found them frozen into a block of ice when defrosting the refrigerator (Admiral Byrd).

"Those must be four or five years old," Jerry had said. "I wondered what had happened to them." And he brought them along. I had sworn off drugs many years before, but had never tried mushrooms. Having read the works of Carlos Castaneda, I felt my curiosity stir. A mushroom seemed so organic. I agreed to try.

An hour later, when I said I felt no effect, Jerry said he didn't either and so we each took another one, slightly larger. After another half-hour, and feeling no effect at all, I said I was going to bed and crawled into my sleeping bag.

I woke to the gods wringing my soul… shivering uncontrollably, I was convinced I was dying and I envisioned Jerry finding me there dead. It was so vivid, I was sure it was really happening. Overcome with sorrow at my own death, I wept. Finally I called out to Jerry. He came into the tent and lay close to me and reminded me I had done the mushroom. I had forgotten. But it did not stop the dying. And dying was not so bad, after all. I had thought earlier, high on the glacier, that it would be a good day to die—up so high and the snow

Cho Oyu, 8201 meters.

so clear and the sky so blue, just to sail into it. I was so happy in my marriage. Death might be a way to live that moment forever.

But the night was different, darker. The night was phosphorescent light, a full moon reflecting off many glaciers. And the darkness came in spurts with rain clouds covering the moon, dark and threatening with thunder and rain. I began to remember explicit details of the Castaneda books—tiny details forgotten by my workaday conscience—of the sorcerer don Juan and the journeys of his pupil. And I understood them.

The mushroom god is a natural phenomenon, which has identifiable characteristics. This may be true of all drugs. They take you to themselves, and the mushroom god *is* the land. What power it has when taken in its own environment. I wandered wonderful, strange paths through the mountains, into the mountains, into the very soil of the mountains, into those parts of myself connected to and part of the mountains and the soil. If the death was necessary for me to go further, that was okay. I understood I was standing at the boundary don Juan asked Carlos to ignore. Difficult. Abraham sacrificing his child. The basis for blood sacrifice? And yet, if it turned out the boundary could be ignored, all would be well. All would probably be well in any event.

The flesh of my body was vaguely aware of Jerry holding me. I concentrated on focusing my eyes, and looked up to find him laughing with tears running down his face, "Now you've got *me* crying," he said, "and *I know* you're not dying."

I awoke later to find him crouched at the end of the tent peering out of the flap.

"What are you doing?" I asked.

"Watching the show," he said.

I crawled over to peek out of the tent. The full moon reflecting off the snow peaks gave an iridescent silver lining to the silhouetted ridge. Dark clouds drifted and stopped, drifted and stopped, pulsating with light. We huddled there, arms around each other, watching the show.

Jerry said to me then, "Let's do have kids."

"But," I started.

"But I never planned on meeting you," he said.

My thoughts were brought back to the present by the acrid smell of the carpet cleaner. Unless the veterinarians came up with some new idea to save B.J.'s life, Jerry's injury wouldn't be the only loss we would have to suffer together. As to children, years of refraining from birth control had not done the trick. Just before Jerry left for Cho Oyu, he had undergone some fertility tests and I had done the same during his absence. The recommendation had been artificial insemination, but it didn't seem like a topic to bring up at the present time. There were other matters of more present concern.

"Did you summit?" I finally asked.

"Bring the picture," he said.

Before Jerry left, he'd met with Wally Berg, a climber who had summitted Cho Oyu. Wally had shared his slide show and given us a photo of the mountain. The huge snow-sculpted massif, distinguished by its pyramid shape belted by a visible band of stratified rock, rose out of miles of lifeless ruble. Above the layered band, and above a layer of clouds, the upper reaches of the mountain curve in a broad, glaciated dome.

"I made it to here," said Jerry, pointing to what appeared to be the crown of the mound, the top of the mountain.

"Looks like the top. It's not the summit?" I asked.

"I made it to 8000 meters. You can't actually see the summit in this picture, it's back over a couple hundred feet."

"Does it matter?" I ventured.

"The damage may have been worse," he said, "yet, I suppose I wish I could say I'd done it."

I understood mountains at some level. I did not understand this. Of course, I had never been above 14,000 feet.

And why did I not follow Jerry up the big ones? One learns early in climbing of the 'false peak.' From below, the contour of the mountain approached is near impossible to discern. Time after time one reaches the 'top' to find nothing but a ridge leading to yet another ridge, which may or may not lead to the summit, which may or may not be the summit one had one's sights on.

Our climbing paths were doomed to split. Early one Friday morning in August of 1985, married four years, I was driving to court. Not a block from the house, as I turned from Mohawk onto Baseline, a delivery truck ran a red light and hit my car just forward of the driver's seat. The vehicle was tossed, crunched, and I stepped out shaken but not in need of an ambulance. I was sore, and hiking that weekend was an ordeal. About a week later, sitting up in the bed trying to find a position in which to sleep that was not excruciating, I realized I had a serious problem.

The next four years for me would be a series of visits to doctors, chiropractors, physical therapists, massage therapists, neurologists, and acupuncturists. I suffered from constant upper back pain and migraine headaches. I tried not to let it slow me down, but it did. Some days I could barely get my coat on. So, when Jerry said he wanted to go higher and planned a climb of Rainier in Washington State, there was no question I would not be joining him. Did I want to

Sunrise on Mount Ranier in Washington State.

Cho Oyu.

go? I never let myself think so; it wasn't an option given my health.

Technically only a fourteen thousand-foot peak, Ranier juts up from sea level, dwarfing most of Colorado's peaks, which emerge at about 9,000 feet. Jerry didn't make it to the top that year, but came back happy with tales of mist and avalanches and with beautiful photographs of the sun rising over a universe of clouds. The next year he tried it again, having cajoled my brother Jonathan into the trip, and the pictures from the summit were even more beautiful. Then he signed up for McKinley (Denali).

"And what did Cho Oyu have in store for the others?" I asked.

"Kent, Cathleen and Cleve summitted together," he said, "Karon was behind them and summitted alone. Dick, Doug and I turned back at 8000 meters."

"Boy, I thought Doug was your strongest climber."

"He was/is," said Jerry, "It's not always about who is strongest. Doug the Animal." He shook his head. Doug the Animal had been climbing with Jerry since Denali.

A Backpacker Climbs Denali

*...[A] man who keeps company with glaciers comes
to feel tolerably insignificant by and by.*

Mark Twain
from "A Tramp Abroad"

When Jerry prepared to climb Denali in the Spring of 1987, we had been married five and one-half years. We had invested in a half-interest in a vacation home in Breckenridge. My back pain and headaches continued, and when Jerry went downhill skiing, I opted for cross-country skiing with the dogs. They are very different sports— one involving encounters with countless people, competitive, energetic in a kinetic way, the other almost a meditation of motion and for me another way to venture deep into the silence of the mountains. Stopping in a rare grove of oak trees, I could hear the snow approaching in the rustle of dead leaves on the winter trees. And then would come the softest sound of all, the snow itself.

Jerry did his share of cross-country skiing as well, but he used a combination ski that allowed him to lock his boots for downhill maneuvers. When he decided to take two-day winter ski trips camping

Glacier on Mount McKinley, Alaska.

in the snow, I declined to join and was grateful for the fireplace and cozy bed in Breckenridge. Anyone sleeping in the snow was crazy. It was 'training,' he said.

Then Jerry found an advertisement in the CMC newsletter. Someone was looking for climbers interested in climbing Denali, in Alaska. He attended the meeting and was impressed with the credentials and experience of the group that showed up, with the exception of a fellow named Cleve.

"You can't believe the different personalities and the incredible differences in people's approaches to climbing." Jerry said. "There's this one fellow named Cleve. What a character. He says, 'my approach to climbing is to bag the peak or come home in a body bag.' What an egotist; how'd you like to have some guy like that on a climb?"

I shuddered. In the CMC courses, I had been offended more than once by the slide presentations of famous climbers who called a climb a 'success' even when their teammates had died in the enterprise. A few days later Jerry was informed that he had been chosen to go. I was relieved to know the fellow named Cleve was not on the climb.

Jerry was the least experienced of the Colorado Denali group, with several others having climbed in South America. The roster included five men and one woman. The group engaged in a number of practice climbs, preparing themselves by skiing in with their gear to set up winter camp and sleep in tents and snow caves among the high peaks of Colorado. As he got on the plane, I handed Jerry a copy, the thinnest I could find, of <u>Moby-Dick</u>, and a miniature ceramic dog, about ½ inch high, who would earn the name "Denali Dog."

On May 25, 1987, the Colorado Denali team was deposited onto the Kahiltna Glacier. Denali, at 21,200 feet, lies near the North Pole where the air thins dramatically. Climbing Denali is equated to a climb in the Himalayas because, though the high Himalayas soar to above 26,000 feet, they sit near the equator where oxygen is more plentiful. No climber would fail to take Denali seriously. The team would be approximately three weeks on the mountain.

The team was kept at base for a couple of days by heavy snows and then began its way on skis up the mountain. Mushing through snow and fog, they arrived at Camp 2—7700 feet—at about 4:30 a.m. on May 27th.

The springtime night on Denali, or lack thereof, confines itself to a few hours from about 1:00 to 3:00 a.m. A dusky twilight accompanied the climb, the dim light combining with the reflection of the glacial snow to make the world a black and white place – like an old tin photograph – with grays almost silver, rock formations hauntingly dark and non-dimensional against a flat sky. The only living things that venture so high, other than crazy men and women, are huge dark ravens. Traveling solitary, they search the mountain hoping for a climber's cache to pillage, forcing all climbers to bury their supplies in the snow.

The first thing to know about climbing is that a big mountain entails many climbs. In the interest of keeping their audiences, the movies on climbing do not focus on the fact that one must acclimatize to high altitude, which means going up and coming down to adjust to the lack

Jerry on the summit of Mount McKinley (Denali).

of oxygen. The body adapts slowly. The average climb of a Colorado mountain, where the altitude is already an influence but not too much of one, is three thousand feet of elevation gain. As one gets higher, one moves slower due to less oxygen. And so it was up and down, carrying caches, setting up camp, moving up.

In a typical day the team pushed a cache, for example, up to 14,100 and came back to camp at 11,000. Seven hours up, two hours down. Jerry was hauling about a fifty-pound load and pulling a forty-pound sled, the "skins" on the bottom of his skis (once made from real seal skin, now a synthetic fabric with a stiff-bristled nap) providing traction, the nap of the fabric catching the snow with the movement of the heel pushing forward, and then flattening down for the glide in a rhythmic pulse broken only occasionally by a jerk of the rope—a team member pausing, stumbling, or breaking the stride to avoid one of the many yawning crevasses, or to squint, trying to discern the path marked by wands left in the snow by those who had gone ahead.

I don't need to ask why Jerry does it. I have had sufficient contact with mountains to understand. When a climber moves, life collapses into each moment, this action, this glide, this push, avoiding this outcrop of rock, this crevasse; occasionally, terrain permitting, one's thoughts arc all the way to the next anticipated camp or maybe even to tomorrow, to calculations of rations or a mental sorting of equipment; but mostly the mind adheres as close to the snow, to the mountain, as the underside of the skis and skins themselves and rarely, very rarely, turns back to the platitudes of life, the flat-lands of mundane modern existence left behind. This distance, this presence in the place and only the place, was what Jerry loved.

They used the skis to 11,000 feet, where the terrain became too steep and the preferred footwear was crampons. Then the rhythm changed from a glide to a click-click as the talons on the crampons gripped packed snow.

The second thing to know about mountaineering is that team politics are everything. On Denali, the team of six (five men and one woman) suffered early from divisiveness.

"We're getting nowhere," said Warren, hunkered down over a stove at 11,000 feet. "We were sleeping higher than this in Colorado." Warren was a type A achiever, an electrical engineer from Golden.

He was here for one purpose and one purpose only, to "summit".

Jerry had never changed his career to the practice of law (one practicing lawyer in the family is enough), but he was never shy about advocating his position.

"But you forget," he said to Warren "we've been sitting on our butts at sea level. We've lost our Colorado advantage. We all need to acclimatize. It is a slow process."

"I say we need to gain more altitude or we're not going to make it," retorted Warren. "Let's ask the marines." He looked at K.C, who was now an architect but had been a Marine, and was the team leader.

"I agree," said K.C., "We're wasting our time down here, I want to see the mountain."

"Okay, let's vote," said Warren.

Donna, a Boulder fireperson, took Jerry's side: "The rule is 'push high, sleep low, and move slow.' We have plenty of time, and remember the fellow we found our second day here? Wandering around the mountain in a mental fog with his boots unlaced. He had pulmonary edema (PE)." She said it just as she would give one of her firefighter lectures to the school kids, in a recitation. "It can kill you and the only known cure is altitude loss. Not worth the risk. Let's acclimatize by the book."

"Mike?" asked Warren.

Mike had been a financial assistant at Aspen but was now out of work. He was also a vegetarian, which had complicated the meal planning no end. He wouldn't even eat chicken broth and objected to anyone else cooking it. At five-foot-ten, Mike was a little pudgy and the slowest of the group in both climbing and getting his stuff together to move it out of camp. Mike also had not invested in equipment as heavily as the rest. However, his ego was intact.

"I'm for pushing it faster," he said.

Jerry just shook his head and glanced up at his friend. Doug, alias "the Animal," was in fantastic shape—five hundred push-ups a day—and was one of the more experienced hard rock and ice climbers Jerry had met. Technical climbing with Doug with like driving an expensive automobile—each movement smooth, precise and dependable—and he could perform all day long. Six feet tall with not an ounce of fat, Doug was a quiet, easygoing, patient fellow, characteristics that had gained him a second nickname—Clint Eastwood. His personality flaw was that he never wanted to cause controversy or disappoint. His standard answer: "I could go either way."

So, the team started out the next day with higher goals—move faster, move higher—but their plans were thwarted. At about 12,000 feet, the group was overtaken by park rangers headed up to the Mesner Glacier to rescue a climber. They asked for volunteers, and Jerry and Doug agreed to go. The rescuers climbed to about 14,800 to help lower a German who had come down with pulmonary edema. This fellow went from 7,200 to 19,000 feet in five days (just as Warren wanted to do), made the summit, and came back down to 17,000 feet. His friends had tried to wake him in the morning and found him unconscious.

With the help of oxygen, the fellow was conscious again by the time they got to the medical tent at 12,000. Lucky. The Europeans have the highest incident of edema problems on Denali. They call their approach to climbing Alpine style –a quick climb up and down. Supposedly it minimizes the risks of being on the mountain for a long time and maximizes the use of weather windows, but it seems to kill people rather quickly also. So, rather by default, Jerry won, and the team agreed to slow the pace.

About a week into the climb, the team switched tent-mates. Jerry had been rooming with K.C., whose need to dictate everything in his military fashion had been starting to get on Jerry's nerves—though eating and sleeping with any stranger for six days is bound to strain the relationship. Jerry, who would now be sharing a tent with Donna, looked forward to the shift. Jerry had done enough warm-up climbs to feel comfortable with both Donna's ability and her personality. As the first woman lieutenant in Boulder's fire department, Donna would later make captain despite the most difficult tests. When she took the physical exams to be a firefighter, the skeptical (and probably a bit threatened, examiners) had convinced the phony two-hundred-pound "victim" to go limp on her. Donna had done fine. She was tenacious, used to teamwork and living in close quarters, and she knew how to keep to herself allowing another person the small privacy a shared tent can provide. She also had the most extensive experience of anyone in the group, having climbed Colorado's one hundred highest peaks and a number of 18,000 to 20,000 foot peaks in South America.

The team had moved their camp up to 11,000 feet and found a spot big enough to put the three tents next to one another. The tent Jerry and Donna shared ended up in the middle next to a VE25 Northface tent occupied by K.C. and Warren. Warren started talking, evidently forgetting the "walls" were membrane thin, about how the "real problem with this expedition is that we have three climbers and three *backpackers*"—K.C., Warren and Doug being the *climbers* and Donna, Mike, and Jerry being the *backpackers*. To Jerry's disappointment, K.C. went along with the evaluation. Warren had experience just about equivalent to Jerry's, and Donna had climbed more than either of them by an order of magnitude. Mike was a different matter, for he *was* slowing the group down.

No doubt about it, the team was breaking into two factions – without Doug's or Mike's knowledge. Donna and Jerry sat quietly in their tent, seething, until Jerry whispered, "Listen, we've got the Aryan, Warren, with a hyperactive adrenaline gland, and Mike, the type B vegetarian. Perhaps if we drained their blood in the night and gave each a transfusion of each other's vital fluids, Mike would move faster and Warren would mellow out." They laughed, releasing the tension sufficiently to allow a night's rest.

In the morning, having come up with a less drastic solution than blood transfusions, Jerry and Donna suggested changing rope teams to put Mike with Doug (who could basically drag him at a faster pace than he was keeping). This helped a bit and the team moved on up the mountain, slowly, over the next few days.

Just past Windy Corner, where the winds tossed some of the smaller climbers around like leaves, Warren tumbled into a crevasse. Huge fissures under the ice of the glacier can be concealed by a thin covering of ice or fresh snow, and though the spot looked solid, Warren's body weight caused it to collapse. The fissure literally gobbled him up. Climbers are lost on Denali every year to crevasse falls; a roped team helps, and the team had their man out quickly, but Warren was wet. The look on his face was half gratitude, half disdain as the climber was forced to accept the help of his shunned teammates before hypothermia set in. Turning around, Donna and Jerry dragged the shivering Warren back to the 14,200 camp. The rest of the team trailed behind. By the time they reached the camp, Warren's body temperature was down to 95 degrees. Donna and Jerry heaved the almost comatose body into a tent, wrapped him is a down sleeping bag and yelled to the others to warm some liquids. As soon as the water on the stove began to boil (water boils at a remarkably low temperature at altitude), chicken bullion was thrown in and the patient was spoon fed broth. Within an hour Warren was okay. Left unattended, he would have died.

After rest, the team once again began their move up to 17,200 feet. Before them stretched a vast coulior and as they started up, a dense snow began to fall. The steep, wall-like slope was composed of solid blue ice with two feet of fresh powder snow on top, making it a difficult go. In addition, the coulior was crowded with climbers. The team got a bit off-route to let a descending party pass and ended up on ice where no steps had been kicked. Each step required using ice hammers with the hands and the teeth of the crampons on the front of the boots to hammer into the ice. They call it front-pointing. Thus, scrambling and clawing their way, they moved upward. Jerry had been keeping his boots loose to ward off frostbite (by improving circulation) and didn't realize that with each step his feet slid forward, hammering his toes against the boots. His feet were so cold, that he didn't feel a thing.

Exhausted, Jerry crawled gratefully into his tent that night. He was suffering not only from physical exhaustion, but from that irritability that inevitably comes with a prolonged lack of creature comforts. Jerry had been wearing the same set of clothes throughout the ten days of climbing. He had one other set, but they were heavyweight and were being saved for the summit attempt. His socks smelled bad, his clothes smelled bad, *he* smelled bad—but so did everyone else.

Trying to distract himself from the scent of himself, Jerry turned his attention to Moby-Dick and chanced upon Chapter 23 and a handwritten note: "Hi Jerry, this is my favorite piece of writing in the English language. Enjoy. Love, Cyndi." A smile creased his face as he read and reread the short chapter, noting in his diary that I must have expected him to have a dictionary. "Apotheosis?" But he knew why I had chosen the passage.

There is a single sentence: "…all deep, earnest thinking is but the intrepid effort of the soul to keep the open independence of her sea; while the wildest winds of heaven and earth conspire to cast her on the treacherous, slavish shore." And isn't a climber's climb a similar effort though of the body—maybe dragging the soul as he'd been dragging his pack on a sled, seeking some kind of independence in the face of the gravity of the day-to-day existence that conspires towards crevasses, conformity, and inaction? Jerry closed the book and fell asleep listening to the warring avalanches above him and the groaning glacier below.

The next morning, with camp settled at 17,200, the climbers were free to make an attempt at the summit. Warren was still shaky from the crevasse fall and K.C., the team leader, offered to stay with him. Thus, only four of the climbers donned their heavier gear and stumbled off for a first shot at the summit – Donna, Doug, Mike, and Jerry. They let Mike lead because he was the known slowest, but after three hours of climbing though a wet snowstorm, the company had gained only 1000 feet. The weather was not improving, so at 1:00 p.m. they gave up.

Returning to camp, Jerry saw a figure moving toward him, as if in greeting, but in a wavering, uncertain manner. He soon recognized the figure to be the team leader K.C., but could he be drunk? No, of course not. Lack of balance at altitude is the first sign of cerebral edema – water building up on the brain. The cure is like that for pulmonary edema – you lose altitude fast, and K.C. did not argue with the consensus of the impromptu team meeting that he should head down the mountain. So, Doug took K.C. down to the 14,200 camp to get checked at the medical tent.

The others settled into the 17,200 camp. Heavy wind gusts, extreme cold, and the sounds of resounding avalanches were not the only disturbances that kept them from a peaceful night. Around 10:00 p.m., some British fellows showed up in the cold, blowing snow and asked the Colorado team if they could borrow snow saws and shovels. They built some snow block walls adjacent to the Colorado team to protect their tents. The resulting complex was like an old walled city– every wall shared.

No sooner had they finished, when some Swiss climbers arrived in camp and it turned out the Brits had built their camp on top of the Swiss cache. A lesson in the language barrier ensued! Say something loud enough, long enough, and everybody understands that nobody is sleeping until the problem is understood and solved. Finally the Brits agreed to move their tents and the camp settled into silence. Jerry drifted into a restless sleep, only to be awaked again by a scratching at the tent.

Doug, the Animal, had successfully escorted K.C. down to the 14,200 camp. The medical personnel there agreed K.C. had pulmonary (as well as cerebral) edema and recommended he move to a lower altitude as fast as possible. A lady climber had taken a crevasse fall and hurt her back pretty badly, but since she was

"Oh my God, there must be a God," Mount McKinley, Alaska.

ambulatory, they paired her up with K.C. and sent the impaired couple down to Kahiltna Base to be flown out. That left Doug at 14,200 feet. About 8:00 p.m. he decided to solo up to the 17,200' camp and arrived nearly frozen about midnight. The scratching Jerry heard was his friend fumbling with the zipper of the tent.

Jerry got up at 6:00 a.m. to temperatures of minus ten and frozen sleet propelled by winds of forty-five to sixty miles per hour– a no go for an early shot at the summit. Reports came in on the radio of a major impending front and Warren decided he was going down for good. Colorado Denali had dwindled from six to four in twenty-four hours, left with three 'backpackers' and one 'climber.'

The faces of a mountain can be fickle, and by 11:00 a.m. the temperature had risen to minus 5 and the winds diminished to 20 miles per hour. That equates to a nice, pleasant wind chill of minus 46 degrees; but the Brits turned out to be training for an Arctic military maneuver, and apparently they thought the weather was just ducky. Listening to the British singing as they packed their gear, the remnants of the Colorado team decided they could not argue with such enthusiasm, and packed their gear as well. Five British soldiers and four Colorado climbers marched off in step for the summit.

Sleeting winds caught up to them again at Denali Pass where Jerry, at 200 pounds, had to struggle to keep his balance, and the team roped up to keep from losing each other in the swirling mists. Finally, at 19,000 feet they popped out of the clouds to see the South Peak of Denali floating before them like an iceberg in the sea of clouds, strangely displaced, a mile away, but tauntingly close. Jerry had heard the stories of climbers just stepping into the void, but only now did he understand how that could happen. Whatever strange faith had led him up to this enchanted place would either swallow him or let him down on clouds. In the meantime, he concentrated on breathing. It took over three hours to go from 19,000 to 20,000 because of the lack of oxygen. One step, three breaths.

Fifty feet below the summit ridge, the group was granted a respite from the relentless winds, and even enjoyed a spattering of sun on their numb faces; but the mountain was only teasing. As they made the ridge itself, Jerry was knocked over, landing face-first in the crusted snow. Emerging from his involuntary face-plant, Jerry scrambled forward, crab-like, his glasses crystallizing into opaque ice. Groping his way half-blind the last hundred feet, the backpacker found himself on the top of Denali.

When Jerry arrived home, he was skinny and complaining about great pain in his feet. "From the front-pointing," he said, calling it 'hammertoe.' The doctors called it 'a touch of frostbite.' Jerry had some simple surgery to remove the nails of the affected toes. He was on crutches for a bit, but all the nails grew in again and by the end of the summer it was a forgotten matter.

Pik Korzchenevskoé in the Pamirs.

Getting By

There are mountainous, uncomfortable days,
up which one takes an infinite time to pass.

Marcel Proust
from "Remembrance of Things Past"

"A touch of frostbite." Should we have known? Should I have prevented him from climbing? Could he prevent me from writing? What a useless question. The only woman I know who actively attempted to intervene in her husband's climbing got a divorce as the door prize. So, what did Denali give us? There are academics who claim that shifting attitudes toward nature rise from cultural assumptions, that a radical shift occurred in the eighteenth century—from mountains as feared objects that distort the harmony of the landscape to mountains as sources of the sublime. The academics derive this interesting perspective from reading literature, studying literature and the perceptions of the literary, in English. And where is the flaw in logic? England's highest peak is Ben Nevis at 4,404 feet. And which of the Isle's fabled literati were real climbers? And so, if the cultured feared mountains, can we not ascribe it to a fear of the unknown? For the knowing have always revered their mountains. The mountain folk are perhaps not literary, but the select who live at above 14,000 feet have always equated their mountains with the sublime. Their history is recorded, not in literature, but orally. The native people call Denali just that—the "Great One." The Sherpas of Nepal believe the high peaks are inhabited by the gods, or actually are the gods (such as Chomolugma—the Mother goddess of the world—also known as Everest). Jerry came home with the "Oh my god, there must be a god" shot. And that's as close to religion as an ex-alter boy is likely to get. And to those who say we are culturally predisposed to view things one way or another, and what we expect arises from the ideas of the time, Jerry says simply, you should take a stroll up Denali, and see for yourself whether it speaks louder than the times. The curiosity is that, perhaps like heroin, perhaps like the mountains of Colorado that spoke to me that night the psylosibin gods wrung out my soul, like burning bushes to some and holy wine to others, mountains speak, and they chose their conversations.

And now the mountains had chosen to converse directly with Jerry's flesh.

"Time for bed," I said, "Let's get your feet done." Every day, twice a day, I knelt before Jerry like Magdalene herself, changing the bandages around the seeping eschar—the back crust of dead flesh. I unwrapped, cleaned and re-wrapped the feet with the efficiency of a nurse.

The next day, Jerry did an accounting and wrote each member a check for around $700 from the money left from the expedition. A couple of days later Kent was the first to show up to collect some of the gear. Kent had a rugged, mountain-man look about him, the kind of guy that could pose for ads for outdoor wear, but his usual confident manner was absent. He shuffled uncomfortably as he handed me an article on frostbite. This was the first indication that the other team members even knew of Jerry's condition. I glanced at the first paragraph; it stated unequivocally that most damage from frostbite occurred walking on the injured feet. I stared at Kent, wanting to ask him why then, why they hadn't carried Jerry out like the famous climber Tichy was littered out in 1954? But why ask now? So I simply handed him the refunds for himself and Cathleen and helped him out with his gear. Jerry had just come out of a day surgery and was sleeping off the anesthesia, so I didn't try to wake him. Cleve stopped by a few days later for his and Karon's stuff. We didn't hear from Dick, or Doug, as if some shame attached to not making the summit, and sent off their refunds by mail. Doug's came back marked 'Moved. No Forwarding Address.'

The days flowed by like sludge. Jerry was at home during this time, the risk of infection and the pain too severe to allow him to go to work. He was on substantial painkillers. He drank and watched television. My days were crammed with the responsibilities of taking care of Jerry and B.J., the dog, who continued to throw up, and my law practice. The weeks passed. Every day I got up, did wound care, went to work, billed, litigated, negotiated, drafted pleadings, left work to run the errands, attend to the lists Jerry created for me of things to be done, came home and cooked and cleaned and bathed and bandaged the feet again. The fingers were healing, shedding the black crust naturally and taking only the tips of two fingers.

We watched television. We'd never watched television much, and I cannot tell you the plot of a single hour of transmission that occurred during that time. We just used it as an anesthetic. It was awful, dead time. Except Saturdays. Saturdays Chris and John came over at 5:00 p.m. with pizza. We watched Star Trek, the Next Generation, and the guys talked computer talk. John had worked with Jerry at one of their computer software start-ups, one that, like so many, had never really started. Chris holds a Ph.D. in flute, and her artistic nature is reflected not only in the lovely music that her instrument produces, but in her dress and demeanor. Jerry describes them as the last of the Bohemians—always colorfully dressed from thrift shops and refreshingly unorthodox in their opinions on just about anything. They barged in like a carnival side show come to town, cheerful and chattering. I was so grateful for their arrival, so happy to toss the baton to John for those few hours to keep a conversation going, so relieved to have a woman with whom I could banter about anything, anything except our situation. For Jerry and I alone, it was getting tenser:

"You go on to bed," he said. "I'll be in in a bit, but bring me another drink first."

"I don't think you are supposed to mix pain killers and alcohol," I said meekly, my father's alcoholism looming before me. I knew alcohol to be the harbinger of ruin to a marriage. Ours was such a fragile thing now—as delicate and sensitive as the baby pink new skin that appeared on his fingertips as the black caps sloughed off. The old marriage had been based on an unspoken compact of self-reliance; although at times I may have yearned for Jerry to say I could quit my job, try writing, I had learned years ago that dependence was not acceptable to him. He didn't pick a housewife; he picked an attorney. He didn't ask anything from anyone else that he didn't expect from himself. But now he had to ask. I was the only one he could ask. He had no choice and I felt like he hated me for it.

"Just bring me the god damned drink," he said, "Nothing else cuts the pain."

"But it makes you so irritable," I ventured.

"Sorry," he said sarcastically, "I've lost my feet and my wife doesn't want me to sound irritable?"

"I'm worried about addiction."

"If I'm addicted, I'll deal with it later. The doctors said that was a possibility. You don't understand the pain, Cyndi. You can't possibly imagine. It is like someone is kicking my guts in—all the time."

Chomolugma, Mother Goddess of the World.

I wondered if he was climbing the mountain a thousand times in his mind, questioning at what point if he had turned around, he would not have done so much damage, wondering …I didn't even know what he was wondering. I didn't even know what had happened, and he wasn't talking.

So I left him and went to bed. I dreamt of feet. I dreamt of the winter of 1812: the damaged men, their horses and dogs walking the frozen Russian continent, beaten by the cold itself, driven backwards, feet and hands black with the insidious death of flesh. I woke feeling strangely comforted, in the company of all those women who had dealt with the same situation I had, and whose prospects for what it meant to their lives were so much more threatening; it meant survival to them and their families. We had the indulgence to worry about psychological impacts. Jerry would survive this. I would survive. The only question was whether we would survive together.

And there were the surgeries. At first they were minor "debredments" to take off the clearly dead parts, but we were moving toward amputations. Several times Jerry was hospitalized for a day or two. During the operations I sat stoically in the waiting rooms watching Oprah, and during the hospitalizations I sneaked in beers and fast food and bandages. Jerry was never happy with the food or the way the nurses took care of him.

"How on earth do you live with that man?" one nurse asked me. Another took me aside to say, "I'm surprised you're sticking this out. Most marriages don't make it through this kind of thing. And yours is a bear to live with." "Yeah," I thought, "Misha"—remembering his Russian nickname.

A Bigger Mountain

Upon my word, doctor, things seem to be worth nothing
by what they are in themselves. I begin to believe that the
only solid thing about them is the spiritual value which
everyone discovers in his own form of activity...

Joseph Conrad
from "Nostromo"

I'd had my own share of pain and hospitals. Four years after the
car accident, the doctors had finally "discovered," with the help of an
MRI, that I had been walking around with a ruptured disc in my neck.
The pain had taken a toll. Unable to bear the two-hour commute to
Denver, I'd found a much less prestigious position with a law firm in
Boulder. Still, I suffered from exhaustion, my body depleted by the
constant pain and the migraine headaches. So, it was with great hope
that I scheduled the surgery for a C-4, C-5 disc fusion for February
of 1989. I was thirty-five, Jerry had just turned forty (at the surprise
party I'd thrown I hired, instead of a stripper, a fellow to show his
slides of a climb of Nanda Devi.)

Within a day of the surgery, I knew it had been a success. The relief was tremendous. I wore a brace for a couple of months and would still have lingering back pain, but it was bothersome, not debilitating, and I would still suffer from migraines; but, by that summer, I was hiking again, though it was mostly with the dogs.

Jerry, at that time, was "training" again, preparing for a climb in the Pamirs, in what was then called the USSR. A group of four was planning a climb of Pik Kommunizma (the name has most probably now reverted to some earlier incarnation), at 7482 meters (24,590') the highest peak in the then Soviet Union. The mountain is located in the Pamirs, with two other 7000-meter peaks, which are on the Afghanistan, China, Russia border. The climb was under the auspicious leadership of Tom, whom Jerry would later dub the "Old Goat." The Old Goat was a year or two older than Jerry and about 5'6", 120 pounds – a little elfish guy, balding, with a fringe of frizzy red hair and a beard. At 43, he had endless energy. He also did not appear to have to work for a living. He did some professional guide work and climbing and dance instruction. The amazing thing is that, with all the free time and the energy of a child and constant activity, the Old Goat never actually got anything done. The result was that the climb, despite having only four team members, was a disorganized chaos from beginning to end. The team started out two days later than their scheduled flight because the Old Goat did not process the visas early enough, and without visas they could not enter the Soviet Union. Eight hours of haggling on the day before their departure produced the visas, but was an indicator that the Old Goat was not one to plan ahead.

On July 12, 1989 the group, having flown through New York to Moscow, and Moscow to Osh, were on a helicopter for a fifty-minute flight to Moskvin base camp, the international base camp located at the edge of the Moskovin Glacier, at 14,000 feet. What a trip! Fifty minutes of one spectacular sight after another. The route is up glacier, up a valley, surrounded by rugged peaks reaching 16,000, 20,000, and 24,000 feet. Just when it was clear there was no room to fly, the pilot managed a 180-degree turn and landed...well, not really. They cannot land. The helicopter came to a semi-stop with engines at one-half throttle and the pilot let the runners barely touch the ground. The loading doors were opened, the climbers threw their gear off and jumped, and the helicopter was gone.

In Russia Jerry got his nickname Misha. He was so named by Valentina, the interpreter appointed by the Soviets. It is Russian for "Little Bear" and Jerry willingly accepted the nickname, thinking of our B. J., the Little Bear of the Sangre de Cristo.

The team consisted of Jerry, Tom the Old Goat, Andy and Doug—yes, Denali Doug, 'the Animal.' If there was any redeeming factor to this climb, Jerry thought, it would be Doug's presence.

Unfortunately, the Old Goat suffered from the same "summit fever" Jerry and Doug had seen on Denali, and arguments ensued immediately regarding the pace of the climb. Base camp was at 14,000 feet. Jerry and Andy wanted to stay put and acclimatize. Doug, consistent with his signature attitude, said he could go or stay. Not the Old Goat. Tom wanted to do a cache load to 16,200 feet on the first day. Finally the Russians in charge of base camp intervened, and required a plan of acclimatization. It was decided the group would warm-up on a lesser (7000 meter) peak called Pik Korzchenevskoé, named after a Czar's wife. None of the team could pronounce the name, so they decided to call it Peak "K."

Then the bad news came. Jerry and Doug had failed the blood pressure tests. For Doug it was particularly weird since he'd never had a history of high blood pressure and was in fantastic shape. For Jerry, it was an age-old problem that whenever someone wanted to take his blood pressure, it went through the ceiling. When he was eighteen the draft board declined Jerry for the army after putting him in the hospital for two days to prove it wasn't some drug he'd taken to mess with his blood pressure for the induction physical. Just the thought of serving in the army in Vietnam was enough to make his blood pressure soar. But now he needed his condition to behave, and it didn't help that, in the hustle and bustle of traveling and time zones, he had forgotten to take his medication. Jerry could not explain what happened. The doctor took his pulse and it was 100; his normal is 60. Then the doctor took a resting blood pressure and it was 160/110. Then he made Jerry do ten knee bends. The blood pressure jumped to 210/160. Nine months of training, an investment of $3200 for airfare and permit fees, and he was grounded. The trip had disaster written all over it.

Jerry and Doug commiserated. Maybe the Russians didn't have accurate instrumentation. Maybe it was just acclimatization; they were living at 14,000 feet when three days earlier they had been at sea level. The two friends went for an unauthorized walk to about 15,500 feet. That's the highest either of them had been since Denali two years earlier. As on Denali, they talked about forming two groups: the "passees" and the "failees." The problem would be that there were a few pieces of group equipment that are required for high altitude—the pressure cooker, high altitude stove—of which the team only had one. So, if Jerry did not pass the physical in the next couple of days, he would miss the window and might as well pack it up.

The two hung around an overcrowded base camp. There must have been two hundred-fifty people and it was noisy and dirty: voices screaming, radios blasting, trash everywhere. The Europeans and Russians do not believe in pack it in/pack it out. They just leave trash everywhere—cans, plastic bags, human excrement. The only entertainment was to watch the Bulgarians at base camp drink amazing amounts of beer and still get up with the sun. Jerry was depressed enough to be calculating how to get home.

The next day, Jerry entered the medical tent trying to curb the apprehension he knew would only make his blood pressure go up. He was clutching Edward Abby's <u>Desert Solitude</u> and asked the doctor if he could read for a half-hour before they took the test. The doctor shrugged; Jerry sank into the calm of the desert and emerged a half-hour later to pass the test. Thank you, Edward Abby. Doug passed

Cold Camp 2 in the Pamirs.

too, and on the 14th of August 1989, they were given the go-ahead to attempt the "K" Peak, their warm-up climb.

Hauling "light" packs of fifty pounds, the two took seven hours to reach 16,400 feet. The Soviet's sense of humor must have been at work. Jerry and Doug were told there would be 3400' of elevation gain, but they weren't told about the 1400 feet of loss, so the total gain was more like 4800 feet. They were told it could be done in five hours. No one mortal has done it in less than six, most take eight, and Jerry and Doug did it in seven. The Russians also do not know the meaning of a switchback. The trail was either straight up or straight down.

The Russian method of climbing is climb high, sleep high, come down and rest – whereas most others climb high and sleep low. Different. So Jerry and Doug slept at Camp 1 and returned. They did not expect to see the Old Goat and Andy, but there they sat.

"What gives?" asked Jerry.

The Old Goat had the pout of a six-year old on his elfish face. "Told us we had to stay and get the team together." Jerry smiled. It took Soviet intervention to clip the Old Goat's wings and force a group meeting.

Their fearless leader had his ideas, as usual. Tom was sick with diarrhea, and hadn't eaten in three days, "That's why we need to speed things up," he said, "We need to get up and down the mountain as quickly as possible before my strength gives."

Nobody agreed. The rest of the team voted for spending a day at Camp I, getting fat and hydrated, then trying Camp 2 and Camp 3 and the summit. The Russians wanted the team to go to Camp 2, spend a night, leave their gear and pack all the way back to base for a day of rest. None of them wanted to return to the nastiness of base and make the ascent to Camp 1 again. This was the first and only thing they agreed on as a team.

After their day of rest, with a crack-of-noon start, the team made the ascent to Camp 2. The gain was a mere 2500 feet with full, very heavy packs. They did it in just under five hours. The last 200 meters (660') was straight up. It alone took two hours.

Camp 2 is referred to as the 'cold camp' because it sits on a shelf under a cliff and does not get sun until about three p.m. but at least they were finally on snow. The climb to Camp 1 had been on dirt and rock, which is difficult with plastic boots. Jerry's feet were blistering. The one advantage to the cold camp was that it held its snow and made walking easier.

That night, sharing a tent with Andy for the first time, Jerry (aka Misha) learned of how bad things were with the Old Goat. Andy was not a complainer. In fact he was one of the most mild-mannered people Jerry had ever met, his friendly, freckled face open and kind, but after almost a week locked into step with the Old Goat he was desperate to have someone to whine to: "That idiot has been bumming lunch food from me from day one. Says he forgot to bring any. *Any*! He borrowed my lip protection and forgot to give it back, then forgot the group peanut butter, hot chocolate, and Jell-O."

The Old Goat had been given group funds for this stuff, and both Jerry and Andy were angry. It wasn't a matter of a few dollars; the Old Goat was jeopardizing the climb and the health of the climbers with daily surprises about what they did not have. Incidentally, if you think go-for-health climber types live on peanut butter, potato chips, Jell-O and chocolate on the flats, think again. The last time Jerry had had any of these items was on Denali, but they are high energy and there's just no way to get green chili and enchiladas up a mountain. Misha was discouraged and homesick.

The revolution officially started at 7:00 p.m. that night when each team was required to radio in and inform the Russians of the plans for the next day. The Old Goat, of course, told the Russians that the team was pushing up to Camp 3. Jerry and Doug had just ascended 4500 feet in two days, which is beyond the recommended 1000 to 1500 feet a day. They were not acclimatized. Jerry insisted on taking a rest day. The Old Goat responded to this position like a bull to a red flag. Andy joined Jerry. Doug, our "Clint Eastwood," said nothing. The Old Goat took this to mean Doug was on his side and started making plans to leave, but then Doug asserted himself and said, "I think I could use the rest." So, there they were – all four of them sitting on the shelf of the cold camp 2.

The Old Goat was given the task of lighting the stove and starting the process of melting snow for water.

"Hey Jerry," he called, "can I have that box of matches you had last night? Mine don't seem to work."

Jerry looked over at him. The Old Goat was pulling half-damp matches out of a Hyatt-Regency matchbook. Jerry shook his head and tossed his own box. Wooden waterproof matches cost a whole 25 cents a box. Bet your life.

But the stove didn't start. It had run out of fuel. The Old Goat, as leader, was to have coordinated who was to carry what. Jerry and Doug were laden with group equipment. They assumed that meant Tom had the fuel and food. Nobody had the fuel. Being low on fuel was no big deal, however, because the Old Goat had not brought the food. There was nothing to cook. They still had to get to the high camp, Camp 3, then go to the summit and finally spend another night at Camp 3. There was some fuel at Camp 1, but hardly enough to make it worthwhile to go and get it. Leaders are supposed to coordinate that kind of thing. The Old Goat had planned not only on eating other people's food, but on using a garbage bag and solar gain to melt snow. Well, it was cloudy. So much for solar gain.

So they sat, hungry and thirsty and tired, at 19,000 feet on "K" peak. Jerry had already made up his mind that if he summitted "K" he would call it a victory, since it was a 7000-meter peak and higher than he'd ever been. Now he was doubtful they could even accomplish that. They would try by pushing up to Camp 3 at 21,000 feet the next day and hopefully summit the day after. The summit is 23,670 feet or so, but is approached by a long, corniced ridge. "If one thing goes wrong – injury, weather, etc., we will be cutting this attempt way too close," he thought, " How the hell did I let myself get into this situation? Next time *I* am the leader or I don't climb."

They got up the next morning rested and eager to move on, only to discover weather had come in during the night. Camp 3 received sixteen inches of snow and the mountain was beginning to avalanche heavily. All personnel from Camp 3 were ordered down to 2, and it looked like the team would have to retreat all the way to base for food and fuel. Of course, the Old Goat had some grand plan to wait it out living on someone else's food and no water. They headed down.

On July 21, 1989, the team members had been on the mountain for two weeks, had ten days left on the permit, and were sitting at the base camp where they started. Two things then happened at base. First, everyone but the Old Goat agreed with Jerry that they should abandon all thoughts of climbing Pik Kommunizma, the higher peak. The visa deadline created a time pressure and produced a sort of deadline fever, even if ten days away. There simply was not time, for no one could assume an easy ascent. In fact, no one had summitted Kommunizma or its sister peak, Lenin, yet that season. The Russians had had a team of twelve on Kommunizma since Jerry had arrived, and they had yet to summit. So, the goal was Pik Korzchenevskoé, the "K" peak itself.

The next crucial thing was that a climber resigned. While at the base camp showers, Andy stated he was going no further with the group. Instead, he would hang around base taking photographs and look for interesting mineral samples. Nobody asked why. Jerry could sympathize. He wasn't far from giving up himself.

The next day it was time to go on up the mountain again. Heading out toward Camp 1, the three climbers took off about fifteen minutes apart, leaving Jerry to climb by himself – oh, sweet solitude. He had been eating, sleeping, climbing, planning and living with the other guys for the last two weeks. What delight to just be alone for awhile, to set his own pace, to pause and look at a scene or rock whenever he wanted to.

The route traversed part of the glacier with little rivulets of cold water running through. Jerry came around a corner, and there sat a Russian climber naked as a jaybird bathing in water which had to be about 32 degrees. Knowing little Russian, Jerry put his arms around his body and made a shivering motion. The bather laughed and shrugged it off. As Jerry walked away, he said "Despedanya." The man returned the phrase and gave Jerry a big thumbs up and pointed to the mountain. How different their lives; how similar their loves.

What remained of the team stayed that night at Camp 1; then it was up to Camp 2 again. Jerry spent a second day of solitude climbing alone through a very pleasant, snowy afternoon punctuated by avalanches going off on either side of him. He was reunited with the Old Goat and Doug as they looked for places to put their tents. Camp 2 was over-occupied with twenty-one tents in an area that could comfortably hold ten. Jerry's Bilber tent was parked on top of what was once the latrine, but fortunately there was about eighteen feet of packed snow between him and the human waste. Jerry was reminded of the movie *Poltergeist*, where they built homes on an old cemetery and came to regret it. Fortunately the night passed without event.

The next morning it was on and upward to Camp 3. There was a group of Russian trainers out in front most of the way who did the majority of the work breaking trail through eighteen inches of new snow. After arriving, Jerry started having stomach trouble—the diarrhea the Old Goat had gone through earlier. The team had dubbed it the Pamirs' plague. Anything put into the body wanted to leave in liquid form about thirty minutes later. Jerry sat miserably in his tent while the temperature dropped from a balmy forty degrees in fifteen minutes to zero Fahrenheit, as the sun went behind a ridge. Listening to the avalanches plunging through the valley below him, Jerry thought of the women memorialized in the book named so appropriately "Storm and Sorrow", who lost their lives on Pik Kommunizma in 1974. He thought of home. He was halfway around the world and while everyone thought he was climbing Pik Kommunizma, he was really about to make a summit bid on Pik Korzchenevskoé. He could die on the wrong mountain.

Jerry rifled through his pack and finally turned out a tiny white polar bear. No bigger than a kidney bean, it was the only piece of surplus baggage he carried. On Ranier he had taken a tiny quartz donkey, on Denali a little ceramic dog, and here, for Russia, was a polar bear.

On July 24, 1989 the polar bear was christened with the name Korzchenevskoé. It would no longer be K peak. Once you summit, it is easier to pronounce. At approximately 4:00 p.m., Doug and Jerry topped the summit. The day had been hard, but pleasant. For Jerry, climbing with Doug was a joy. Their pace was similar and there was no whining, just a knowledge of each other's presence and strength. The avalanches were quiet. The two men let the Old Goat go ahead of them, and by the time they reached the summit he had gone, leaving them to themselves and a beautiful view of snowpeaks in static waves as far as the eye could see.

The Peak is 7105 meters or about 23,680 feet. That's about 1000 feet less than Pik Kommunizma, but for as lousy as Jerry felt about the whole endeavor, it would do just fine. He could say he'd climbed a 7000 meter peak, clearly the highest and the hardest peak he'd climbed, in more than one way.

All three made it back to base camp. Not quite the way Jerry would have planned it, however. They slept at Camp 3. The Russians informed everyone in the daily 8:00 a.m. radio contact, and via some trainers who were up there, that Camp 3 was being evacuated as of 9:00 a.m. because of a major storm front. They had been getting 60 +mph wind gusts from 7:00 p.m. the night before and it started snowing

On the summit of Korzchenevskoé.

heavily at about 6:00 a.m. The weather forecast was entirely correct, creating two problems. The first was that Jerry and Doug had come back from the summit, drunk a cup of soup each, had a little water, and that was it. There had been no time to get re-hydrated. The second problem was trying to break camp in a blizzard and a raging blizzard at that. But there was no alternative.

It is commonly acknowledged that more people are hurt going down than going up a mountain. Jerry knew that, but he was tired and trying to move fast because of the weather. The snow was about knee deep as he reached a short rock rib—an exposed area of rock projecting from the mountain. For this pitch, someone, probably the Russian trainers, had put in a piece of fixed rope. On the way up, Jerry had not bothered using it, but, knowing he was tired, he decided to clip in with a carabiner—a locking metal clip that attaches climber to rope. After the first step, he decided he'd better put the ice axe leash around his hand. On the second step, his crampon glanced off a piece of rock and he found himself suspended out in space looking straight down about 1000 feet with his ice axe dangling off his arm and his butt slamming into a piece of rock. The fixed line had kept him near the face, not allowing him to be propelled into space. He recovered in seconds, using the fixed line to maneuver back to safety, but they were the longest seconds he'd ever lived. A strange loneliness overcame him as he clutched the rock, recovering from what his heart had clearly been convinced was a life-threatening situation. What was that quote from Carlos Castaneda...? "[a]n immense amount of pettiness is dropped if your death makes a gesture to you." Jerry's death gave a top o' the morning, but didn't stay to strike up a conversation, and the loneliness ebbed into mild euphoria.

The avalanche danger had been building by the minute. Jerry followed Doug down a rock rib to a long traverse, and then the trainers insisted Jerry go second behind one of them. They wanted him to break trail, but they also wanted him, with his weight, to trigger the slough avalanches. It worked—with every step snow groaned and broke beneath him.

Once the traverse was done, the trainers took over. They were on another traverse with a fixed line when an avalanche triggered above them. The wall of snow was coming right at them. What to do? Put your head down, dig in your ice axe, and kiss your ass good-bye. It worked. The thing went by and there they stood, the two trainers, Jerry, and Doug, all still attached to the fixed line.

They arrived at base camp about 4:45 p.m., having started about 8:45 a.m. It was not the longest day of Jerry's life, but combined with the day before, it ranked right up there. One of the base camp trainers walked up to Jerry to tell him he had witnessed the fall, complimenting him on a really nice recovery. What a bizarre combination of isolation and lack of privacy. One falls alone; with no resources but one's own strength of muscle and mind; one recovers (or fails to recover) alone. And yet, across a valley, far from any possibility of intervention, someone may be nonchalantly witnessing your triumphs, or your very demise.

When Jerry got back to Base he got a chance to look at his feet for the first time in five days. Somehow he had managed to sever a huge callus from the left big toe. He treated it with a topical antibiotic and taped it up, hoping to make it home or at least down the mountain before dealing with it; but by morning, Jerry knew he could not ignore the toe. He had taken three Tylenol-3's to get through the night. He found a Russian medic, a woman named Tanya, who offered to help. She commenced the surgery without washing her hands—grabbed a scalpel and scissors, numbed the toe with some spray stuff, and started cutting. Jerry ended up with a hole on the outside of his big toe about the size of a half-dollar. That made for a rather interesting situation since, once they dressed the wound, he could no longer put his boot back on. Anyway, the doctor said a boot would not be good; Jerry should let the thing breathe.

Since he wasn't about to cut a hole in plastic boots or his hand-made hiking boots, something needed to be created. Sasha, the Russian trainer, who had a PhD in physics, came to the rescue. Not that it takes a PhD in physics to figure this one out, but he found a board, put the foot on top of it, etched an outline of the foot, and cut the board to fit the foot. He then wrapped the board in gauze and tape and created the sole of a Moskvin custom sandal. Then, with the help of some more gauze and a stretch net bandage, the sole was attached to the foot.

They weren't scheduled to fly out for several days, but the threat of Jerry's foot procured the team a ride on the first helicopter flight out to a lower base camp, one they'd avoided coming in. They were promptly met by the base chief – they had a chief for everything over there – who looked at them blankly and stated, "Your departure is scheduled for August 2." They were stuck at Ackitash Base for one full week.

"But I need medical care," said Jerry.

Waiting to leave the Pamirs.

"Everyone could say that," said the man. "You will wait your turn."

Jerry could not walk normally, let alone put on a pair of plastic boots. And then the Russians changed their minds.

Part of it might have been that Jerry went to get his toe checked and the doctor recommended he lose altitude, if he could, to prompt healing. They were currently living about 12,000 feet. The injury was better, but the whole toe had turned purple. The doctor said it looked to him as if Jerry had frostbite. Jerry thought he was wrong, but asked him to make it official and tell the chief, who reluctantly issued the passes for the next plane.

Their fellow passengers were some young Russians who had been on Pik Lenin. One girl had frostbite of the lips. Jerry cringed thinking of the weeks and months of recovery she had ahead of her and wondered if they have plastic surgeons in the USSR. Talking to the other climbers, Jerry confirmed that the success rates on the 7000 meter peaks in the Pamirs had been dismal. No one other than four trainers had summitted Pik Kommunizma. Fewer than twenty had made it to the summit of Pik Lenin, and that peak had taken the life of a local trainer. Jerry and Doug were sad at the news, but were pleased that they would be leaving Russia with a "pik" to their credit, even if its name was Pik Korzchenevskoé.

Drinking from the River Nepenthe

Quaff, oh quaff this kind Nepenthe...

Edgar Allan Poe
from "The Raven"

So, Jerry's feet had always been his Achille's heel; and I shouldn't be surprised. I grabbed the dressings from the nurse who had just dared to insult my marriage, and moved into the room where my husband waited. There was never a question I would see Jerry through the healing, though I was beginning to feel a deep trepidation as to where we would be afterward. If he turned sullen and sour, would I be able to take it? Well, I could take it for the moment. I knew Jerry didn't see me at all right now—not separately from himself, and his criticism was not really directed at me. He could ask of me what he could not of others, and expect it done. Such is the promise and the seduction of marriage, the glory and the shame: that the two will be one. For a decade we had been together—like quartzite, that hard metamorphic sandstone so firmly cemented that, if it were to break, it would do so through the grains rather than between them; if we lost, we neither of us would walk away whole. But the alcohol worried me.

I began to watch his consumption like a weatherman tracking a typhoon on radar. I measured the depletion of the bottle in inches. The gin bottles started as ½ liter, grew to liters and then Jerry figured out how to get the liquor store to deliver—1.75 liter bottles—by the case.

I did not underestimate the substance's power. I'd seen booze seep insidiously beneath the foundation of my parents' marriage and buckle it—bedrock turned to bentonite, overnight—and when bentonite is introduced to moisture, it starts to heave, and the cement slab foundation built upon it, cracks; the instability reverberates throughout the entire building, cracking the walls, undermining the integrity of the entire structure. I know; I litigated a bentonite case once. The Denver-metro area is riddled with bentonite…and, I dare say, alcoholics. But lawyers can argue either side of any argument, so I rationalized. My fears derived from my upbringing, and I'd done a pretty good job of eliminating the influences of the past on my present. Besides, Daddy Paul drank Jack Daniels. Jerry drank gin. Clear alcohols—the vodkas and gins—aren't like the bourbons, the whiskeys, the ryes, whose color and casking age into them not only the flavor and hoary odor of men who have done indescribable things under their influence, but the very demons of incivility and irritability— proved to have escaped into the consumer by their witnessed escape by way of the consumer's vitriolic tongue.

By the time my father stopped drinking, my mother had discovered channeling—a form of meditation whereby one invites or allows spirits from the other side, dead people—to invade (occupy?) one's body for purposes of communicating. She believed adamantly that Dad was possessed by evil spirits, i.e., demons, and that alcohol opens one's spirit to such occupation. She paid to have him exorcised in abstentia.

But, my rationalizations argued, clear liquor does not necessarily equate to the more monstrous honey-colored drinks. A glimpse at the ingredients on a Bombay bottle produces sufficient evidence to convince any jury that the liquor contained therein is of a different essence altogether: Coriander from Morocco, Liquorice from China, Lemon Peel and Almonds from Spain, Angelica root from Saxony, Orris root and Juniper berries from Italy, and Cassia Bark from Indo-China. Does that sound like the kind of potion that would encapsulate demons? Genies, maybe. Too exotic, too sensual for demons. I was beginning to indulge myself and, with the help of this delightful concoction of Oriental herbs, to find a bit of solace. I needed a bit of self-administered solace. Comfort surely was not coming from others.

My role was to play nurse. I was the only one who could do it. For Jerry, life itself was a battle unarticulated—I sensed a cavernous desire to give in to the weakness, to dissolve, to disappear, to avoid the pain and the very fact of injury through the morphine, the Percocets, the Tylenol-4's, the gin. Jerry was crouching under my college Chautauqua tree with a rusty razor. I knew that. I was crouching there with him. On more than one night I used the liquorice aftertaste of Bombay gin to mask the bitter taste of one of Jerry's pain killers as I swallowed the pill; not because I had a migraine; just to obliterate, temporarily, the pain of us.

On December 18, 1991 I stood in Court prepared for a full day hearing. The Judge called me into his chambers.

"How is your husband?" he said. Judge Brumbaugh was a tall, thin man who easily could have played the role of Sherlock Holmes. His face had that kind of reserve and intelligence. Although he'd come to his position through political connections, he was not the kind who flaunted them. He had a careful, considered approach to the law and treated lawyers courteously. In a tough legal world where pride, ego, prejudice, or connections too often determined the result, Judge Brumbaugh's court was a safe haven of actual application of law to fact. I prepared for my cases before him meticulously, but respected his decisions, pro or con, to my client.

"We're scheduled for his amputations at 5:00 today," I said.

"What the hell are you doing here?" he asked.

"It's not until 5:00, "I replied. My voice held no emotion. I felt no emotion. I had evidenced no emotion for months, not to Jerry, not to anyone else. I looked quizzically at the Judge, "If I don't have my work," I said, "I have nothing."

"We'll reschedule," the judge said shaking his head, knowing more about where this thing sat in my life than I did, "now get out of here."

I left the Courthouse and drove to a camera shop. It was a week before Christmas and I had not purchased a gift for Jerry. I thought I'd look at a camera lens. Maybe he'd get more into his photography now. He'd always said he'd like a dark room. One could operate a dark room in a wheel chair, couldn't one? In my desperation to do something that would give Jerry back joy, I overspent. The startled assistant helped me buy all the components of a dark room: enlarger, trays, paper, and chemicals. "This is my dream," said the young man, "want to adopt me?"

As the shop fellow loaded the mountain of photographic equipment into my car, I felt the nausea rise and knew I had better get home. I'd suffered from migraines since that car accident in 1985, but this was a bad one. The Boulder\Denver Turnpike was a blur. Stopping by home to feed the dogs, I swallowed two Percodan before going to the hospital.

"How are you doing?" I asked, squeezing into the cubicle they called a hospital room. At least tonight he wasn't sharing a room. That always made him even more irritable.

"I called Bob the hair cutter and asked if he could do me a favor and make a house call here. You know what he said?"

"What?"

"He doesn't do hospitals. The guy calls himself a friend of mine, and I ask him a favor. He doesn't do hospitals."

"We've lost a lot of friends," I said. "Or perhaps just discovered who our real friends are."

"Like frostbite is contagious?"

"Or bad luck. Where the hell are your teammates?"

Jerry remained stoically silent. I was feeling relaxed now, due to the two Percodan, and mean.

"They all managed to show up for their gear and refunds," I said, "always managing to pick a time you were in the hospital or unavailable. Clairvoyant. Oh, there's a letter here from Doug."

Jerry opened the letter and laughed—a dark laugh.

"He's pissed that he hasn't gotten his money back. He never gave us his new address."

"I don't suppose any of them thought of offering the money to help with our medicals?"

"Right," was all he said.

Then they came to take him to surgery. I left the hospital that night after he'd come out of the anesthesia. I always waited to make sure he came out of the anesthesia and had his pain under control before leaving. The morphine dispenser attached to his IV let him administer to his own pain. It seemed to keep him calm.

That night I sat at home, nestled in front of the wood-burning stove watching a blowing snowstorm plaster the windows. Throwing another log into Buckie Fuller (in our home even fireplace insert wood-burners have a name—Buck was the brand), I noticed a discoloration where the Tibetan ring encircled the finger. The skin was copper green—a color I knew well from my collect-rocks-because-Daddy-is-a-miner years. Cheap. It didn't matter. It was beautiful all the same—the same number of hours go into casting the cheapest of silver as the richest grade—no refection on the artist. And what would I do tonight? What memory conjure out of my past to bring comfort? I was running out of yak dung. And then I remembered the Liard—Oh River—if I have been granted a river Nepenthe in my lifetime, it is the Liard, quivering in my memory, suspended like a hawk on a thermal—wings barely fluttering.

It was after the Pamirs, before Cho Oyu, just a couple of weeks in heaven.

"Andy is a great guy," Jerry said, "and he and his wife are taking a raft and canoe trip in the Yukon. Let's go with them."

"I can't swim."

"No problem," he said, "the current is too fast to let you swim. If you ever fell in you'd hit your head on a rock and drown, or die of hypothermia in the river."

"Great," I said and together with Andy and his wife, we flew to Juneau, Alaska, stopped just long enough to see the heaving walls of blue glacier ice that define that town, and boarded a ferry to take us up the Inner Passage to Skagway. That ferry ride is to mountain lovers what the Great North Woods in fall must be to tree lovers—an ocean of peaks, a granite wonderland iced in snow. On the upper deck the sun was intense enough to bake out of my taut muscles the stress of almost ten years of lawyering.

At Skagway we met the other four members of the group, who had rented a van in Denver and driven up the ALCAN Highway with rafts, canoes, and provisions. The vehicle had been a brand new Ford van; it already looked like it had been through a war with the paint blasted off by road debris. They'd taken out the seats to accommodate the rafts, canoes, and gear, and when we loaded six of us into the back, it was clear the shocks were gone.

"Got the car rental insurance package," said Andy grinning his friendly, freckled grin. He seemed to have recovered well from the disappointment of the Pamirs climb. He explained later, "I wanted to climb Kommunizma because a friend of mine died on that mountain. When we turned to Peak K, I just didn't have the stomach to put up with the Old Goat."

"I can relate to that," said Jerry, and they opened a beer.

"What do I do if I fall in?" I asked, stepping with trepidation into my first canoe.

The Liard River, Yukon Territory.

"Stand up and breath normally," Jerry yelled over the splash as I stepped into the gunnel and flipped the canoe. He was right. The water wasn't but waist deep. The rest of the team was howling. We'd driven into Teslin, Yukon, to be met by Denny Dennison of Coyote Air Services. Denny had flown us and our canoes and rafts into a small alpine lake, landed on the water, and dropped us on shore. From there we would wend our way, first in canoes, then in a combination, using the rafts as the reedy streamlets became streams, then bigger streams and then rivers, tributaries which eventually fed into the great Liard River.

There had been tremendous flooding that spring, and in numerous places the river had actually changed course, ripping trees and creating dams, forming new islands, new river channels. We were humbled by the evidence everywhere of the force of the flooding, by the sheer height of the trees, by our distance from civilization. The Colorado mountains were tame compared to this wild and untouched country. Ten days we went with the only evidence of man being some red paint scrapes on rocks in a shallow of the river.

I learned to paddle, to avoid rocks and "strainers"— the sieves along the side formed by fallen trees and floating plant debris. If a canoe gets swept in, the debris and limbs can trap it underwater and those in the canoe can drown. Listening to Jerry's commands, my paddle flipped from side to side until the three of us, man, woman and canoe, were a single instrument of navigation wending through white water.

One evening Jerry and I were just floating in the canoe, ahead of the rafts by about a half-mile. The gray shadow light of evening lingered long in the Yukon mid-summer. It was our favorite time of day for spotting wildlife as the animals came down to the river. We'd had to paddle hard to escape a huge, antlered moose that decided to charge our little floating vessel. My favorite animals had been a family of ermine romping in a field of wild strawberries at one campsite. The beavers were plentiful and liked to move close to the canoe, so one could feel the full impact of the splash of water from their slapping tails. We'd seen a wolverine, and Andy had seen a bear. The closest I got to a bear was the fresh tracks I noticed as I squatted to pee on a little island where we'd stopped. I didn't turn around to see if he was still there.

Jerry whispered my name, and as I turned I saw the young wolf eyeing us from the shore. Fascinated by the red canoe, the inquisitive canine loped alongside us for about a half mile, darting in and out of the huge spruce trees.

I tensed with the curiosity of the beast. My muscles were his. The natural world cast its net of drugless magic letting human senses perceive, if only for a moment, the earth in perfect relationship—there was no distinction between Jerry and myself, or between us and the water, the dimming evening light, or the misty eyes of the wolf cub.

As we drifted, I tried and failed to find any way to articulate the feeling, the emotion, to express my joy, my sense of wonder and inclusion in the marvelous. Finally, I turned to Jerry and said simply, "Will you marry me?"

A resonant laughter echoed down the river channel and he said, "Any time."

That trip sings in my mind like a single, suspended violin note—high and never ending, clear and ever calming. I had saved it for this most difficult of nights.

At 7:00 a.m., I returned to the hospital. It was about 10:00 when the hospital sent a woman to take Jerry to get his feet soaked. I followed the wheelchair to the physical therapy room, a sterile, white-tile room full of metal contraptions and whirlpools. The one window looked out to the flat roof covered with white stone. The room seemed to blend into the colorless snow-threatening sky. The only contrast was a large black raven sitting on a silver vent on the roof.

The woman began the process of unwrapping the blood soaked bandages. I felt Jerry's hand grip mine as he looked down at the short stub of each foot, the hamburger-raw, exposed tissue. The physical therapist turned away, embarrassed. Then we all three stared at the raven while the feet soaked. The bird was polite enough to stay for the twenty-minute ordeal.

I arrived home that evening to find a client dragging a Christmas tree from his car, a fellow I had represented in a tangled farm bankruptcy case about onions—600 pounds of onions. When water gets to bentonite beneath a building, the earth heaves. When onions are left in the ground in an early, deep frost, they rot. People litigate over these things.

Phil's cowboy boots and slight ole boy twang belied both his astute business acumen and his generous heart.

"How do," he said, "I figured you wouldn't have gotten around to a tree."

He was right; it was almost Christmas. I scurried around and finally found the stand in the shed. With Phil's help, I put the tree up in the living room so that when Jerry came home two days before Christmas, it was to a tree hung with the old familiar ornaments from those far-off Saskatoon days of my childhood. Christmas day itself was sad, but at least we were home. Jerry sat in the one leather chair with the footstool as I brought out the assortment of wrapped funnels and printing paper, trays and thermometers, sponges and paper cutters. But the expression in Jerry's eyes didn't change. He smiled wanly. You can't buy your way out of despair, and the purchases made with such hope, are tainted. It would take me nine months to pay the balance of the credit card. Nine years later I would give the unopened equipment to an aspiring young photographer I'd taken through bankruptcy. She accepted it with grace and set up her perfect darkroom in a battered trailer home, with brand new, decade old equipment.

We have no pictures of that Christmas. Jerry took a few, but I threw them away. The lines on my face made me look ancient and cruel. I realize now they were just the lines of grief—an upside down "U" on the forehead—described by Darwin as universal within the human species. The muscles themselves know how to grieve even if the person is too stubborn or stoic to recognize their condition. Stoicism was the order of the day for both Jerry and me. We weren't inclined to religion and were rather short on hope.

A New Year

There is advantage in the wisdom won from pain.

Aeschylus
from "Oresteia"

Healing is a slow process. Granulation is the formation of a small, granular mass of tissue on the surface of a healing wound. The scabs that form must be constantly removed to allow the granulation to continue and the wound to eventually close, but when removing the scab material—a particularly painful enterprise given the tender new nerves servicing the regenerated tissue—it makes the wound temporarily larger. And the healing of the soul is no different—two steps forward into the light of a new and confusing reality, and one step back into the vertigo of haunting memory, regret and fear.

To keep the pressure off the new tissue, Jerry would be in a wheelchair for four to six months. Our routine had changed. Now we removed scar tissue, soaked and re-bandaged the feet every morning and night and watched for infection.

"How are you feeling?" I asked, carrying the forty pounds of water from the bathtub into the living room. I was discovering new muscles in my arms and they ached.

Jerry didn't answer, but lifted himself from the wheelchair into the recliner as I attached the electrical stimulus probes to the sides of the footbath. The current was supposed to promote cell growth. I unwound the bandages and he put his feet into the water.

"Christ, " he screamed, "It's too hot, get me cold water."

"I used the thermometer. It should be the same as yesterday."

"Just get the damned water," he said curtly.

I did.

"And can't you find a better towel than that one, it's a rag."

I did.

"Can you bring me those insurance forms?"

I did that.

"And some coffee."

I was grinding the coffee beans when I heard him yell, "You don't have to pulverize it." Why was he always so damn critical? I couldn't even make coffee right. He liked his coffee strong. Tipping the ground coffee into the filter, I stopped halfway. I watched the thin brown liquid drip into the cup and brought him the coffee and painkillers, the vitamins.

"You call that coffee? What about the newspaper?"

Every morning, after I had his feet soaking, I took the dogs across the street to get a newspaper. I loved this brief interlude of minutes that were free from the pain of the house and his criticism, my tiny respite. That morning was bitterly cold, blowing a sharp wind in my face. I had no ability to do anything right, to make it better for him. But his criticisms were over trivial things. I knew he didn't mean for me to take them personally. I let them go and turned my face into the cold wind.

Beneath the trivial response to being criticized, what did I really feel? Alone and naked. Anything not firm in my life had loosened like talus in a landslide; the skeletal personality that was left was not adorned by flesh or by fantasy. Habits of exercise, of reading, even writing in my diary, had been suspended. Friendships I thought would be lifelong had proved transient. I had written to friends to tell them of Jerry's situation, expecting comfort, expecting warmth from them; but the mailbox was devoid of personal letters day after day and had remained so month after month. I realized with sorrow that it was I who had attended to the maintenance of my so-called friendships, and that, left unattended, they had no integrity of their own. It was I who, seeking their approval, had attended to them. Most of the major decisions of my life had been based on proving something to someone—someones who achieved their status in my life because of the respect I afforded them. I'd even become a lawyer to make my statement, prove my strength, to impress whom? Ghosts.

To lose what is ethereal anyway should be no loss, but I felt overwhelmed with loss and I felt angry. And I'd been wearing my anger and self-pity like a shield against Jerry's and where the two angers clashed—there lived our quarrels. But here was revelation—to properly allocate my anger was within my power and it did not mean a return to my old pre-Jerry habit of turning my anger on myself. I pulled my glove off and looked at the old scar across my wrist. I did not regret a single day of my life. Our life together had been wonderful, I could live without false friends, and now my path was dictated for me: just work sufficiently to pay all the bills and attend to him. And there was a strange comfort in this revelation. For the first time in my life what I was to do each minute of each day was absolutely clear, absolutely without choice. It was like being in the army during a war, or in a concentration camp, or perhaps believing in a dictated faith, or like climbing at really high altitude. Place one foot in front of the other, breathe deeply and heave the mass of your body one more step up the mountain. There was no room for questions. The existential refrain of "who am I?" had been silenced.

I felt the slap of first snow on my face and felt joy; knew at the deepest level that I was alive. Only in contradiction to the dark pain and depression of the house across the street, was the emotion so clear—ecstasy.

Loading yaks on the Tibetan plain below Cho Oyu.

I handed Jerry the newspaper, knelt, and put my head in his lap. As he stroked my hair, he said, "I am so sorry for what I have done to you. I'm afraid it's irreparable."

"No," I said, "It's okay."

And one day, finally, the mailbox produced.

"Well, look at this," I said, handing Jerry a filmy blue envelope, the international kind that folds the writing paper into the envelope itself and has delightful Sanskrit letters. "A letter from Nepal."

"Deepak?" Jerry asked. Deepak Lama was the agent who had negotiated the team's business and travel through Nepal.

"No. A single name—T-a-k-c-h-o-e"

Jerry's voice broke. "Takchoe. (Talk-ch-o)" It was the first inkling of emotion I'd seen since his arrival home—the first crack in his stony facade. "Takchoe, the yak herder who gave you the ring?"

"Read the letter," Jerry said, and I did:

Dearest Sir,

Hope you have enjoyed your expedition to Cho Oyu. I am very sorry for long term silence. I am Takchoe. Do you remember? Of course, you do. I am your favourite yak man.

I promised you I will come to Nepal or India as soon as possible. Now, I am in Nepal. From my village to Kathmandu it took two solid months and ten days. In real case, it take two or three days only. I came by walking through Cho Oyu to Namche-Bazaar, over the Nagpa La.

I faced lots problems under border customs. They need lots of money, with reason that I have no passport. To you I am grateful because your gift of money only can allow me to pass. From my heart and soul, I would like to say thank you very much.

I arrived here in Kathmandu with empty pocket. Anyway, I am happy to save my only life. I am very interest to continue my study but I face the financial problem. As you know, my parents and relatives are suffering under Red Chinese. So they can't contribute. They only fill their stomachs and suffer under Chinese cruelty.

I think I should find some job so that I can earn few money. But problem is, I don't get the job of dentist. My hobby is to do trekking. So I may find the place for my hobby. And what is your suggestion regarding my job? I believe you. Thank you.

Yours sincerely, Takchoe.

Friendly beast.

"What a charming fellow, I remarked. "Dentist?"

"He's the one who gave me the ring for you—had been in France studying to be a dentist and had come home to Tibet to work for the summer when he got thrown in jail for speaking English."

"You mean like our dentist schools? That takes years."

Jerry laughed and I realized my husband had been somewhere very different—a place where people starve under political oppression and fifty dollars can buy freedom.

His other mountain adventures had been geological—adventures of his body and physical mountains. The Pamirs had had a cultural aspect, but it was subdued by the strict control the Soviets had maintained over the climbers in their realm. This was different. Jerry had something to share he had not yet shared and not until the arrival of this flimsy piece of paper had the door of that world swung open into ours.

Finally, Jerry let me take out the slides I had processed months ago, so I could see this interesting Tibetan fellow, Takchoe. The lighted image revealed a youth with dark skin, a broad native nose, long hair tied up with braided knots of many colors, a disheveled look that probably only means poverty but carries with it an exotic wildness, obsidian black eyes and a wide smile with good teeth. He looked to be in his early twenties, and behind him stretched the most

Takchoe the herder.

Yak herders find temporary shelter in the ruins of Kytrek.

desolate scenery I'd ever seen—rock debris with an occasional gray nettle plant and, on the horizon, the shape of Cho Oyu, the Turquoise Goddess. "Yu" is the turquoise stone, revered by Tibetans for its healing qualities. "Cho" is goddess.

Moving a load across stream.

Speaking of Goddesses

No leader can foretell which members of a party
will be steadfast in emergency and which will not....

Raymond Lambert
from "White Fury"

Sometime after the holidays, after the letter from Takchoe, Jerry
got a call from Cleve.

"There seems to be some controversy," Cleve said. "Jerry, we've
got someone claiming that Cathleen and Karon weren't the first two
American women on Cho Oyu. We were relying on you telling us
Vera Komarkova summitted under Czech flag."

Apparently there was some confusion in the paperwork and Vera
Komarkova carried an American Flag despite her refugee status in
the United States, making it unclear if Cathleen was the first or second
American woman to summit.

"Karon would like to know. Cathleen is furious," said Cleve, "some
newspaper's saying ..."

"The climb was not about getting the first American woman on
Cho Oyu," responded Jerry. As you will recall, you'd all signed up

before anyone even mentioned it. I heard Vera climbed as a Czech refugee living in the U.S. from Elizabeth Hawley. That's good enough for me."

"Well, we think you should get involved," said Cleve.

"Ask me if I give a damn," Jerry said.

Some team. And Jerry had tried to be so careful. The climb was in the planning for well over a year – in fact Jerry's first query was written to the Chinese Mountaineering Association in November of 1989 – an implementation of Jerry's decision after the Pamirs trip that he would be the leader on his next climb, the master of his own destiny. After the Pamirs, and with the inevitable yearning for 8000 meters, Jerry had selected Cho Oyu, sixth highest peak in the world, sitting on the border of Tibet and Nepal. The climb would be from the Tibetan side under Chinese permit. Everest, with its crowds and trash piles, did not interest Jerry, but he wanted to climb something in the Himalayas.

Obtaining the permit was a great deal of work. Finally, in August of 1990, it was granted for a 1991 climb. The permit was the first granted an American team by the Chinese and could not have been achieved without the hard work of my sister, living in Beijing, raising three children with her husband, a Korean. With the skill acquired living in China for years, an infinite patience with bureaucracy, and relentless persistence, she visited and re-visited the Chinese Mountaineering Association until the task was complete. The peak had been climbed through Nepal, but that route requires an illegal entry into the Tibet side to obtain to the only approach that had proved successful to date.

The plan was to fly into Kathmandu in Nepal, travel overland into Tibet, and hire yaks to help get the gear onto the mountain. The arrangements with the Chinese had been extensive and were complicated by a strike of the Nepal customs agents. In the nick of time, we'd been informed of the strike and had shipped the majority of the gear through Bejing, several thousand miles from the climb. A lot depended upon whether the Chinese kept their promise to have the gear meet the team in Tibet.

Jerry had screened his fellow climbers carefully looking for maturity, experience, and common sense. The final team consisted of eight Colorado residents, none of whom were youngsters. Jerry as leader was forty-three, and his co-leader Kent, a scientist, was near fifty. Kent's girlfriend, Cathleen, was forty-one, and worked as an accounting manager at a health club in Vail. She was blonde and a bit preoccupied with her looks, but she and Kent had climbed together in India, and Jerry thought having couples on the team might add a cohesiveness absent in his other climbs. At least some of the crew would be used to putting up with each other's idiosyncrasies. Dick, a professor of astronomy at the University of Northern Colorado, had climbed with Kent and Cathleen. Cleve and Karon, another couple, were both in their forties. Cleve was an optometrist but had been an army Colonel and Karon was a physical therapist. At first Jerry refused to entertain the thought of having Cleve on the climb. He was the applicant who had said, "I'll bag the peak or come home in a body-bag; it's the summit or a shroud," when applying for the Denali climb. Jerry didn't subscribe to that philosophy and didn't want anyone on his team who did. But a number of years had passed, so Jerry returned Cleve's call.

"I was younger," said Cleve. "And I appreciate life a lot more now."

Jerry believed him. Partially that was attributable to Karon, a deceptively petite, calm-but-not-shy, uncomplaining woman with a sinuous strength. The couple were like oil and water, aggression and complicity, but seemed to work together. They'd climbed in South America and Nepal. Jerry said Cleve could join the team on one condition, that he acknowledge Jerry as leader. Cleve agreed.

Alannah, thirty-nine, was a technical writer, a Boulderite with whom Jerry worked. She had climbed extensively in Colorado and had been in the Pamirs. And there was Doug who, at thirty-eight, was the youngest in the group. This would be the first shot at an 8000-meter peak for each of them.

They met at our house just before departure to assure themselves they had planned for everything.

"Okay," said Jerry, looking around, "Where's Alannah?"

"Saw her today, said she'd be here," said Cleve.

"It's 8:15. I said 8:00" said Jerry, but the doorbell rang and it was Alannah. Jerry's irritation was quelled.

Dick was the most concerned. He had been in charge of food calculations.

"Let's go over it one more time," he insisted, pulling out his paperwork; but all he got were stares from the others. They'd been over and over the rations, what would be bought in Kathmandu. The food had been shipped months ago.

"I think we should talk about Sherpas and oxygen," said Cathleen.

"I don't believe in oxygen," Jerry said, "You've all known that from the beginning. What's the point of pulling yourself up to 8000 meters if you have an oxygen canister that fakes your body into thinking it's at 7000 meters? What's the point? And we talked about hiring some Sherpa people. China requires full fee, and nobody was willing to put up the bucks at permit time. Anybody changing their mind now?"

He looked around the room. No one responded.

"Okay, so it's no oxygen and no porters or guides," said Jerry, "Now, Wally Berg, who climbed Cho Oyu a couple of years ago, gave us some of the photos from his climb, so take a look. You can see the rock band where we hope to put Camp IV."

"Boy, this is almost real," said Cathleen.

"Better be real," said Doug. Everyone turned around. Doug hardly ever spoke, so when he did people paid attention. "Can you see the ice wall?"

"No," said Jerry, "are you concerned?"

Doug laughed, "You think I'm concerned?" Jerry laughed also, "Of course not."

Buddha Eyes.

"Just ready," said Cleve. "Ready to go get us some mountain."

"Well, let's go over the route one more time here, then I've got some news."

They laid out the photos and the topographical maps and charted their climb. Then Jerry announced, "I wrote to Elizabeth Hawley. For those of you who don't know, she's the chronicler of climbs for Reuters. She says…" he hesitated. We'd talked about whether he even wanted to share this news. This team seemed good, but even good teams are lightly glued together, and there is no room in a team effort for personal exaltation. "She says," he repeated, "that Vera Komarkova climbed not as an American citizen but as a Czech refuge. That means if one of our three ladies makes it"—he nodded toward Karon, Cathleen, and Alannah—"she will be the first American woman on Cho Oyu."

There was a perceptible change in the excitement level of the room. Cathleen looked at Kent, who grinned. Karon looked at Cleve, who couldn't control his reaction, "All right, I mean far out, I mean hot damn."

"All right, well, see you in Nepal," Jerry had closed the meeting.

Any time the challenge of climbing an 8,000 meter peak is undertaken, it is done knowing there are risks. These risks are present on any mountain, there is just a better chance of encountering them the bigger the mountain is. Many of the team members of Americans on Cho Oyu were damaged by the cold and the altitude; but I, unfortunately, suffered severe frostbite of the fingers and feet. Since returning from Nepal, I have undergone four surgeries resulting in the amputation of my toes and the portions of the bottoms of my feet. The fingers have mostly healed.

Many climbers have paid a much higher price for the privilege of being on a mountain. I have been wheel chair bound since returning, but recently have taken to walking short distances, measured in feet rather than my usual miles. Cyndi, family, friends and individuals we have met as a result of my injuries have been a tremendous help during this long arduous time. We thank you all.

We hope to climb together again.
Jerry

Friends

Silent friend of many distances
feel how your breath is still increasing space....

Rainer Maria Rilke
from "Sonnets to Orpheus"

"Why aren't they coming around?" I asked. Jerry knew of whom I spoke. The absence of his team members was as palpable a reality in our home as was Jerry's presence.

"We all know what happened up there," he answered. It was all he would say. But for me the time had come to search deeper. I'd been eyeing his diary since the day we got the gear. The battered magenta Spell-Write Steno Book lay on the hutch—unopened. Perhaps within it I would find out what my husband seemed so reluctant to talk about.

The first pages are filled with the beginning of the journey, the beautiful Oriental people on the plane: Koreans, Thai, Indians, a Buddhist monk. Quiet, polite, amazed at someone who is 6'2", standing a shoulder above them. Jerry and Dick flew out a day ahead of the others to deal with money exchange, immigration and customs and the next pages tell of troubles getting the radios through customs in Bangkok. Finally they arrived in Kathmandu, a city that outwardly resembles Boulder—nestled up next to foothills, with great peaks just beyond—but internally is a convoluted maze of alley-streets accessing a population of millions of the world's poorest yet most beautiful people.

At the airport, Jerry wondered irritably why the agent, Deepak Lama, had not met him. Swarmed with entrepreneurs in all sorts of vehicles willing to take them to town, for money, Jerry made his way to the phone. The Kathmandu airport is fairly modern with mahogany ceilings and marble floors, but there is only one phone – spaces for eight, but only one hooked up. Deepak did not answer; his helper, Pasang did.

"Where is Deepak?" Jerry asked.

"At home, where are you?" the voice responded.

"At the airport."

"No," said the voice, "you come tomorrow."

"No," responded Jerry, "we come today."

"You are at the Kathmandu airport?" The voice was beginning to sound concerned. "Today?"

"Yes," said Jerry.

"No," said the voice, very confidently, "you come tomorrow."

"Oh," recognized Jerry. About that International Date Line. Pasang, the voice on the phone, showed up a half an hour later, shaking his head at the silly gringos.

In Kathmandu, people drive on the left-hand side of the street and share a middle lane for turns and passing, from either side. The result is a big, and constant, game of chicken. Honking is a declaration of right of way and diesel fumes pour from the strange three wheel motorized rickshaws Jerry dubbed the 'Darth Vadar' machines. Add the splash of the bright saris worn by the women walking and riding on the back of every motorcycle, and the result is an inundating cacophony of sound and color.

The Tibetan Guest House was not expecting Dick and Jerry until the next day either, yet they found a room with a shared bath…on the fifth floor. A child of eight or nine shouldered a seventy-pound duffel and started up the stairs; he would be ready for Everest at a very young age. The two climbers settled into their rooms and went out to see Thamel. Opting for $10.00 to $13.00 a day rooms instead of the $120 fancy hotels downtown, this is where most of the expeditions and trekkers stay. Percussive Nepali music mixed with the laughter of schoolchildren, the call of roosters and crows, and the horrible shrill sound of stray dogs fighting. In the maze of storefronts and alleyways, one can easily get confused. I had warned Jerry not to wear the tie-dye T-shirt; but he wore it anyway and found himself trying to courteously turn down offers of marijuana and hash along with the regular fare of Tiger Balm, musical instruments, shoe shines, and assorted trinkets.

Jerry and Dick stepped into Alice's Restaurant. Jerry stared at the menu. It offered Nepali/ Chinese/ Mexican/ Italian/Greek and American (hamburgers) food. Jerry thought they'd be eating Nepali later, so he tried the Mexican. Cooked with the same spices (cumin and coriander) used for the Nepali food, and the same strong cheese (yak), using an unleavened Nepali bread instead of Tortillas, it was amazingly palatable, though untraditional for Mexican.

Dick got a few drinks in him and let his inhibitions loose. "I don't know," he said, "I was thinking it over on the plane. I think we've underestimated the fuel."

"Let's not second guess ourselves now, Dick." Jerry replied.

"Well, I'm concerned. Perhaps if we shifted the route…"

"We're not shifting any routes, Dick," said Jerry firmly.

"We could eliminate one of the camps," suggested Dick, "Stage from Base all the way to…"

"Calm down, Dick. We've planned the climb already," said Jerry, "Chill out. You just had too much time on the plane to start rethinking it all. We're cool."

Dick silently went back to his beer, but a few minutes later, it began again.

"Maybe we should have put out for a Sherpa."

"Because we are going in through China, they wanted a full permit fee for a Sherpa guide, Dick. The team voted it down. You just have to trust we've got it together." But Jerry knew Dick was right to be concerned. The shops of Kathmandu were full of expedition gear from climbs too ill organized to even get out of the city.

Jerry was confident. He had spent two years on this climb and had studied the routes to the best of his ability, which included talking Wally Berg and Magna King, each of whom had summitted Cho Oyu, into showing him their slides. He'd read Tichy's version of the 1954 first ascent of the mountain. He had spent endless hours negotiating by letter and fax with the Chinese about how many trucks, how many yaks, how much fuel, and so on.

The first day in Kathmandu, the agent Deepak Lama called Jerry to get the paperwork moving to have the radios released from customs. A car was sent around to fetch Jerry and Dick at the Tibet Guest House, and they were climbing into the vehicle when a woman stuck her head into the car and, with a clipped voice and a very proper attitude, inquired as to whether they intended to be climbing Cho Oyu. It was Miss Elizabeth Hawley. She had come to Kathmandu in 1960 as a stringer for _Time_ magazine, arriving only ten years after the Nepalese borders were opened to climbers and a few years after the first tourists were allowed to enter Nepal. Over her career of more than thirty years, she came to be considered the preeminent chronicler of Himalayan expeditions to Nepal and Tibet.

"Would you be available tomorrow morning?" she inquired.

Jerry said, "sure."

"Well then," Miss Hawley responded, "I'll be round at 9:00 o'clock."

As Miss Hawley walked away, Jerry turned to his driver, Argun: "How on earth could she know who we are?"

Argun responded, "Nobody comes, nobody goes without Miss Hawley knowing."

Jerry called from the other room and I got up to administer to whatever his need might be.

"I'm reading your diary," I said, somewhat cautiously. He didn't seem to respond negatively, so I continued, "I've just met Miss Hawley."

The face of the Sphinx brightened. "She drove up to the guest house in this 1950's Austin Healy Minor and tells me…" Jerry tried to imitate the precisely articulated voice, "I've had to borrow Sir Edmund's car. My 63 Volkswagen is in the garage." He said it again, "gaa-raa-ge," and laughed. "You've got to write her biography, Cyndi. She is the most interesting woman I've ever encountered. She meets with the leader of every climb and knows every detail of every route. More than once, she's had to inform people that she can tell by their descriptions they did not actually summit."

"Has she ever climbed?"

"No, I don't think so. She writes about it." A woman after my own heart, and to her I was *so* grateful. I'm sure this celebrated journalist has been many things to many people. I will remember her as the one who brought the breeze of first laughter into the stagnant environ of our changed life, who, by her image alone, allowed the past to begin its move into our present. Hawley and Takchoe—unlikely, but welcome visitors, tendrils of the real world stretching into our darkness, relieving, if only momentarily, the monotony of our tense relationship and lives— and from across the borders of time as well as continent.

Buddhist temple in Kathmandu.

Approaching the Turquoise Goddess

K'un is the Southwest, it is the earth,
that which is level, fields are there/
Ken is in the Northeast, it is the mountain,
that which is steep; there it is lonely

I-Ching, 39 Chien/ Obstruction

During these months and months, we did not ask what the final result would be. Jerry was still in a wheel chair but for how long was unknown. The original doctor, trying to save what he could, had made poor choices, leaving toe bone stubs which later acted like knives, piercing through the new formed tissue and causing wounds that would not heal. We moved on from specialist to specialist, many of whom recommended transmetatarsal amputations, cutting farther back and losing the metatarsal heads of the toe joint. Physical therapists recommended against this at all costs for functionality; but, whichever way we went, additional surgeries were necessary to take out the bone spurs.

I immersed myself in Jerry's diary:

"Can you give us some landmarks?" Jerry asked Argun, the man Deepak Lama had appointed to help them negotiate the shops of Kathmandu.

"Look for Kytrek. Everything is measured from Kytrek."

"What is Kytrek?"

"Old village."

"And what of the ice wall? Any suggestions?"

"It is maybe 120 feet vertical. Take a good, long rope."

Jerry got as much information out of him as he could as they traveled from shop to shop. One goes to one shop for fixed line, another for food containers, another for kitchenware and kerosene stoves. In the middle of settling on a final price on pots, Steve Miller's tune "Fly Like an Eagle," came blasting out of a boom box in a window across the alley.

The rest of the team arrived that evening. All went smoothly; everyone felt fit and strong, all group equipment and personal equipment arrived. This last alone was an accomplishment, given the recent customs strikes that had forced the majority of the equipment overland through China. Everyone felt the team was a good one. Hopefully it would hold up on the mountain.

That night, having dinner on the rooftop of the guest house, they toasted. "To the mountain," said Jerry.

"To the first American woman on Cho Oyu," said Cathleen, which brought a startled reaction from the rest; arguably she meant to refer the team effort, but nobody took it that way.

Alannah laughed nervously. Cleve bristled and Karon rolled her eyes.

"To the mountain," Jerry repeated, and they all toasted.

The next morning, Deepak Lama called to suggest they accelerate the schedule and leave the next day. There was news of mudslides closing the road at Kodari, on the Nepal side of the Tibetan border.

Just as they were going to board the bus, Jerry noticed a little shop selling toilet paper—real toilet paper. Third world toilet paper is more like compressed cardboard. There had been some discussion as to how much toilet paper would be needed. Dick had said eighteen rolls, but Jerry said that with three women you need twenty-four. So, they'd taken a team vote and decided on twenty-four, but their hurried departure had prevented anyone from getting it. Jerry stepped over to the shop and paid ninety rupees, approximately $2.00, for six roles of deluxe toilet paper—a very expensive purchase in Nepal. Then they packed into a bus and were on their way.

It was August 30th. There were indeed problems with the road. As the bus entered the foothills the trouble began. The road had washed out in a number of places, making the driving precarious, and finally the bus came to a total halt. Jerry followed the other passengers off the bus to find himself in a crowd of people. Doug was pointing at Jerry and grinning: "He's the team leader," he said to the man standing before him. The crowd turned their eyes to Jerry. They were all talking at once, but of course it didn't matter since they were speaking in Nepali. Finally one man appeared who spoke a halting English. There had been a massive mudslide. These were local hill people who, if a price could be negotiated, would carry all the gear over the hillside, around the mudslide.

"But how do we proceed from there?" Jerry inquired.

There was a "trapped" bus that would take them to the next mudslide where more porters awaited their arrival. Free enterprise at work as one barters for the cost of the haul. The negotiator got his price. Nepal is that way: although there is some barter, a shopkeeper is just as likely to look at you and say, "it is a good price," and refuse to barter.

Finally they looked down into a valley and saw a village, Kodari, the last Nepali village before the Tibet border crossing. They found a "hotel" where a village woman crouched over her corner fireplace to produce a marvelous meal of daal-bhaat (rice and lentils) for dinner. Bhaat means both "rice" and "food" or "meal," which is indicative of how often it is consumed. They drank a spiced tea with milk and chang, a pulverized, fermented rice drink stronger than beer but weaker than its distilled form, roxi, which is almost grain alcohol. The team was in good spirits. Then the rain started. The hotel was crude at best, but the roof didn't leak and the dirt floor offered a place to throw a sleeping bag.

In the morning, the team boarded another bus to cross from Kodari to Zhangmu over the Friendship Bridge, which, built by the Chinese, spans a gorge of approximately two hundred feet. As they waited in line at the customs station, they were approached by a stocky middle-aged Chinese man shadowed by a younger, gangly fellow. The older man stopped abruptly in front of Jerry and began to talk aggressively in Chinese. The younger man politely let him finish and then addressed Jerry, "I am interpreter, Huang Ming. I like you to call me Abraham."

"Abraham?" inquired Jerry, a bit surprised by the choice of name.

"Lin Cahn," said the young man.

The young man sported just a bit of a beard and his long angular features gave him a sound resemblance to another Abraham.

"Oh," Jerry laughed, "Abraham Lincoln,"

"My favorite American," said the boy.

"You are a college student?" Jerry asked. Abraham was about to answer when the older man spoke sharply in Chinese. He clearly wanted to be in control, but was forestalled by the need for an interpreter. It seemed to make him angry. Abraham grew serious.

"Liaison Officer says we must talk about the budget," said Abraham. "Also, Liaison Officer does not want to stay here tonight as planned. It is early. Perhaps we can make it to Tingri." Abraham was an intelligent fellow who was studying engineering in Beijing and wanted to learn American history and politics. Jerry was impressed with his openness. After all, this was the China that, not two years earlier, had engaged in the suppression of students in Tiennamen Square. The team would be grateful for his presence as an intermediary. The Liaison Officer was dubbed 'L.O.' immediately and was liked by no one. But it was the L.O. who was urging them forward.

The team, all for progressing further, loaded onto jeeps for a ride over the world's highest and probably most dangerous highway. A few hours later, they stopped in the middle of nowhere at about 17,000 feet, having crossed onto the Tibetan Plateau. The verdant hills had given way to an austere, high-desert landscape, marked only by a few sparse nettle plants.

Abraham jumped out of the Jeep in which he rode with the L.O., and ran back to Jerry's Jeep. "This is where we stay," he said. In response to Jerry's look of shock, he added apologetically, "L.O. says."

There was no food. There was no housing. Nothing.

"This is unacceptable," Jerry said, "we want to go to Tingri."

"Not enough time," came the reply, while they sat and lost time arguing about it.

"We can go to Nylam," said the L.O., "a little further, but you must pay for food and lodging."

The team had already pre-paid to stay in Zhangmu. They had already paid to stay in Tingri. They were doing neither but were being asked to pay more. It seemed like a set-up.

Jerry said "No way" to more pay, realizing that if they got off on the wrong foot now, it would be an endless venture into the pocketbook.

They ended up in Nylam. Jerry told the L.O. there was no money to stay there. It was a standoff, a contest of wills, but better to find out the rules early while other civilization is around, Jerry thought. While the L.O. was fuming, Jerry wandered over to sit on a rock wall. He was approached by a local Tibetan who spoke English.

"You are climbers," the man said.

"Yes," Jerry replied.

Typical camp on the mountain.

"I am approved by the Chinese Mountaineering Association to house climbers."

This Tibetan approached the Liaison Officer and that appeared to appease everyone. So they all sat down to a great meal of daal-bhaat and vegetables at the enterprising Tibetan's house and watched the sun set. The Chinese have the entire country on Beijing time, which means that in the far reaches of Tibet, the sun comes up about 9:00 a.m. and sets at 10:00 p.m.

The next day they passed through the small town of Tingri Dzong and, to their delight, were reunited with the seventeen boxes they had shipped from the United States months earlier. And then it was on to Chinese Base administered by the Chinese; this is where the trucks stopped and the L.O. and Abraham, the interpreter, would stay. Other teams would congregate there and their Liaison Officers and interpreters would also stay. To this end, each team created their own "camp" by carefully placing their tents. Jerry's team chose some circular stone ruins for their camp. Karon was throwing up before the tents were even pitched.

The first order of business was acclimatizing, which means nothing but existing at 16,500 feet and hoping one's blood and bones get used to the lack of oxygen. They put Karon in the Gamow Bag (a chamber which imitates lower altitude by increasing oxygen) for thirty minutes and it seemed to help. They then put Kent in and the bag broke after fifteen minutes. Kent was very sick. Dick was throwing up and blaming it on food he ate two days ago. In short, there were problems. If things did not improve, they would be sending people down.

Jerry holed up in his tent and thought about the plan. They hoped to move fifteen yak loads up to 18,200 feet over two days. Three climbers would go up, five would follow with a second load. The lead three, including Jerry, would come back to rehabilitate from the effects of the altitude gain, probably in four days. That is, if anyone was going anywhere.

Jerry turned his attention to fixing the Gamow Bag. Fortunately it was a minor problem, and that evening Karon, Cleve, and Kent each spent one hour in the bag. That lets you know what Jerry did (the bag requires pumping while someone's inside). Jerry himself felt a little queasy but was holding down food. When he wasn't pumping, Jerry was politicking.

Administratively, the L.O. had come up with about $500 in unexpected fees already. Jerry figured he had a purpose other than to keep the gringos from consorting with the locals: to squeeze them for what they had already paid for. The team agreed to some fees and contested others during a few heated discussions. Then there were problems with the fuel – it didn't burn. The team supposedly had 150 liters of white gas and 40 liters of kerosene, but the white gas was not white gas. Rather, it appeared to be some sort of solvent that would burn in the higher camp stoves, the MSR XGK's, but not in the base camp stoves. This could be a problem.

Jerry asked several people, including the Liaison Officer, but no one seemed to know where lay the mysterious village of Kytrek, from which all else was measured.

By the next day, Cleve and Karon were doing much better, but Kent (on his 50th birthday) was still quite sick. As with the first days at sea, one must just endure. The boredom was relieved with the appearance of some yak herders, local tribal Tibetans with their dark and prominent features and their long black hair braided with colorful stands of string, and their yaks, equally as colorful, wearing collars of braided wool from which brass bells hung suspended. The Tibetans stopped in after dinner for a cup of Chia (tea). There were two of them, and one spoke a few English words. From gestures and their few common words, it was determined that they were going to help the Taiwanese team that was two to three weeks ahead of the Colorado team. They camped nearby and Jerry drifted to sleep to the ding-a-ling of yak bells.

Ding-a-ling all night long. The novelty wore off in a hurry, but the morning brought good news. The team was feeling better, and all eight of them were eating together at breakfast for the first time since they had arrived at Base Camp. It was time to start moving up the mountain. But again there were politicks. Eight drivers and twenty-four yaks showed up when they had only requested five drivers and fifteen yaks. They were to go up, come back and go up again, all over about a six-day period. Luckily one spoke English quite well. His name was Takchoe. The young man proved an able negotiator.

So, the team spent the day getting organized for the yak loads. The team was doing a great job, and everyone was doing his part, with no complaints. It was all a team leader could hope for; however, it did seem to Jerry that for twelve hours a day he had to tell the others what to do. It was tiring.

That night, Jerry retreated to his tent. It was not yet September 1. The yaks would reappear at Advanced Base on October 10; the jeeps would show up at Chinese Base on October 13 to take them home. Realizing it would be some time before he would see home and family, Jerry took the time to find in his gear the "little things" backpack. There was a miniature dog that would accompany the climb and earn the name "Cho Oyu" if he summitted. The tiny backpack contained the little animal, two stones that would be put into new wedding rings, a cassette of me singing, and a tiny envelope that read, "Do not open until September 19". Our anniversary. Seventeen more days. He took out the Walkman and cherished a few minutes of nostalgia. It was a song I'd written for my brother Jonathan's wedding:

> *May it be the higher places*
> *That you seek your greatest joy,*
> *The columbine clings to the alpine rock....*

Jerry noted in his diary how truly unfair it was for him to miss our tenth anniversary.

The next morning brought relief—Doug, Alannah, and Jerry were able to head out with five yak drivers and fifteen yaks. The three worked their way up the valley with each yak carrying two duffels or boxes. The terrain was high desert, above timberline, and the vegetation consisted of nettles. Looking across the vast moraine, Jerry was concerned that they had not seen anything of Kytrek, the abandoned village they expected to see. Absent this landmark, it was hard to know where they were or how high. Jerry thought ironically they might have to wait until the summit to calibrate the altimeter.

It was pleasant to be separated from the Liaison Officer and even the other climbers. All Jerry's time since leaving Kathmandu had been consumed either managing the others, taking care of the others, or responding to concerns over the rations, the fuel, the route. To walk alone was itself a relief.

Near the end of the day, Doug and Jerry guessed they were probably at 18,200 feet. So, they parked the Himalayan Hotel, a tent that holds three people and all their gear. This would become Advanced Base, serving as tent and as headquarters for the climb. There were only 10,000 more vertical feet to the summit and a month to climb them. This sounded quite doable.

Every day the monsoon rains started by 2:00 p.m. and quit around 6:00 p.m. On the way hauling a load up mountain, Jerry, Doug and Alannah had encountered two stream crossings, each about twenty-five feet of rushing glacier water. To cross, the climbers had changed into sandals and used ski poles for balance. Jerry had lost feeling in his feet about halfway across. Rain and the day's snow melt could only make the current worse, and Jerry wanted the three to be past the streams on the way down, at all costs, by 2:00 p.m. before the rains thickened the stream.

To this end, he told them the night before to be ready for a 9:00 a.m. departure. Jerry was ready at 9:00, but despite his best coaxing he could not get the others to move. Jerry picked up the trash, put away the group stove, stored 200 liters of fuel, put his pack together, and noticed Alannah was still filtering some water.

"We've got to move, Alannah," he said.

"It's the altitude. I'm moving slow," she responded.

Jerry paced. By 11:00 when Alannah finally started putting her pack together, he decided he was either going to lose his temper or take off on his own. He chose the latter.

Venturing the stream crossing by himself, Jerry used his ski poles

It was easier for the yaks.

to help balance himself. Mid-stream one of the poles collapsed, throwing him off. As his death winked at him, just before he caught himself, he thought, "I am stupid to be here by myself." If he had not been able to regain his balance, the current would have swept him away, and no one would have known where to even look for the body. A bit shaken, Jerry marched back into Base Camp. By going at his own pace, he had turned a four-hour hike into three and a half. He beat the weather by about fifteen minutes.

Doug had waited for Alannah; they had left the upper camp at 11:20 and had taken their time. The rain started at 2:30. They reached the first stream crossing at 3:00 o'clock. Doug staggered into camp about 4:00 o'clock in a freezing rain. He was hypothermic. Jerry sent Kent and Dick out to find Alannah. They found her stopped on the other side of the stream.

"I'm not crossing," Alannah said.

Kent tried to encourage her, "Come on, Alannah, you can do it."

"I can't do it," she whimpered.

The rain was relentless by this time, and Kent was getting cold and wet. He was not in the mood to be risking his own hypothermia for Alannah. "Don't be absurd, Alannah, you can't stay there, and nobody is coming across to carry you."

She didn't budge, so Dick decided to try a softer tactic. "We've got soup on at Base," he said, "now just do it one step at a time."

Alannah shut her eyes and put her already freezing feet into the frigid glacier water. She opened her eyes again in a hurry with the shock and kept them glued on Dick's face. She was also hypothermic by the time they got her to camp.

The next morning Doug was very sick. Jerry had been climbing with Doug for six years and had never known him to get a sniffle. Kent and Jerry put him in the Gamow Bag for an hour, with no positive effect. Alannah was fine. God protects children and fools, some say. Jerry blamed himself. Should he have demanded more vehemently that Alannah get moving? He felt he had risked his best friend's health and jeopardized his chances at the summit by trying to be accommodating.

Two climbers, Kent and Cathleen, moved up. Jerry stayed down to work Doug through the Gamow bag and get everything organized for the second two-day yak push to High Advanced, or "Advanced Advanced" Base as Jerry dubbed it. High Advanced Camp was only 700 feet higher but 3.5 miles closer to the mountain. When a team is moving over a ton of equipment and food, this is important. This one haul with the yaks would move about 800 pounds of that ton. Some would be left as a cache and the remainder would be moved on the backs of the climbers.

After leaving, the team would not visit Chinese Base for over a month unless a medical problem arose. Jerry would also be leaving behind the Walkman and tapes, which were too heavy. He put his big camera away and looked at the Walkman. He decided to spend the final hour awake listening to the tape. My voice with a rendition of a Marti Jones' song:

> *This has to be the best one yet—*
> *A singing telegram from you in Tibet*
> *Did you really think I'd come?*
> *Drop everything and run....*

As the morning of September 9, 1991 dawned, Doug was coughing up pink phlegm. Jerry and Alannah were pinned down playing nurse. The others had moved on. Alannah approached Jerry, "Can't we leave Doug with Abraham?"

Jerry simply said, "No, he's our climber, our responsibility."

Alannah looked surprised. "You mean you would jeopardize an entire expedition because one person is sick?"

Jerry responded unequivocally, "Yes."

Alannah looked at him in disbelief.

Then Jerry added, "But I am not jeopardizing the entire expedition, just your and my chances of reaching the summit. The expedition is going on, loads are moving, things are getting done."

Below, Alannah and Jerry tended Doug. Above, Karon and Cleve, the closest thing the team had to medical personnel, were informed of the situation by radio.

"We could lose him," Karon confided. Each member listening through the static was silent for a moment, each no doubt feeling the fragility of the human condition, their own inability to help. In the mountains, particularly the highest of mountains, a situation can go from status quo to live-or-die in a very short time. The body can reject its relocation to altitude and simply explode, building up fluid in the lungs or the brain until the person literally drowns when on solid ground. Karon's advice was to get word to the outside, if possible.

Jerry conveyed his concern to the Chinese who told them of a monk passing through Base Camp on his way to Lhasa. Jerry intercepted the fellow to ask if he could send a fax to the United States. The monk said yes, and Jerry wrote a note to me warning of Doug's condition, asking me to contact Doug's girlfriend. How could someone help from the United States? But a person attempting to do something about an emergency feels better than one waiting. At the bottom of the scribbled note, Jerry added a "P.S. Happy Anniversary." It wasn't a singing telegram from Tibet, but it was a facsimile, and that was close. The monk, robed in saffron, took off, headed for Lhasa, in his tennis shoes.

While Alannah took a turn at tending Doug in the Gamow bag, Jerry turned his attention to rearranging some of the personal duffels to adjust for weight. He opened up Dick's duffel to discover five rolls of deluxe toilet paper. He and Alannah laughed until they cried. No one had seen the precious stuff since Zhangmu. The girls had been asking.

Sitting there at Chinese Base, over tea, one of the older yak herders pointed to the walls and said "Kye-trak." The old stone walls that enclosed their tents *was* the village. Dick and Jerry had noted days earlier that the two big piles of prayer stones in front of the camp must

Prayer flags mark the high pass.

have some significance. Now Jerry realized it was their missing reference point.

The next morning things were improving as it looked like Doug

Cho Oyu from the Nepal side.

would recover. Jerry had just gotten off the radio with Karon. The advanced team was at High Advanced Base. Takchoe, the head yak driver, had come through with eleven yaks and moved twenty-two loads to High Advanced Base. Very wet snow was reported up top. Kent was at Low Advanced Base with Dick and Cathleen.

Jerry was sitting in his tent writing when he heard yak bells. He quickly donned his boots and discovered it was two yak drivers and their animals on their way up to meet another team. Quick negotiations and $70 US later, they had loaded ten boxes and two duffels onto a couple of unloaded yaks. Things were rolling.

Doug was looking much better, so he, Jerry and Alannah started up the mountain. By that evening, the full team was together at High Advanced Base Camp. The weather was cool and a light snow was falling constantly. The mountain above them had been obscured in clouds since their arrival and did not deign to make an appearance for them now.

Cho Oyu

*The barrier between me and the rest of creation was
broken down. The few phenomena, sky, ice, rock, wind
and I, which now constituted life, were an inseparable
and divine whole... I had broken through a metaphysical
barrier.... the doors were all thrown wide open and an
indescribable, impersonal bliss filled me. It did not
prevent my believing that we should all die that very day.*

Herbert Tichy
from "Cho Oyu"

It was September 15th and the team was finally setting up Camp
I at 19,600 feet. The climbers were each hauling group food, fuel,
and equipment, which would be used for Camps II, III, and IV. And
so the hauling routine began, as it would continue for two weeks of up
and down, up and down, with fifty-pound packs. The weather
continued to be a mixture: snow at night, sun in late morning/early
afternoon, followed by snow. There was no accumulation at the lower
levels, but rumor from others was that there was plenty up top. A
group from Taiwan pulled out after having spent five days at 26,000
feet. Too much snow kept them from the summit.

Finally, during a late morning break in weather, the shrouds of mist lifted, and the team saw the summit for the first time since crossing the Tibetan plateau. The mountain loomed before them—the rock band a necklace of granite gracing the pure white throat of snow above—waiting, with its dangers, with its rewards. The team was silent, each member engaged in his own practice of geological physiognomy—trying to know the character of this mountain by its face. Everyone was anxious to give the hill a go. She had been tempting them with better than average weather. Jerry had been pressured by some in the group to move faster, but knew the need to acclimatize and the risks of not doing so. It must be approached with patience. They hoped the break in clouds was an indication that the monsoons were abating and there would be clearer weather as they approached their summit attempt.

Cleve and Karon pushed through to establish a Camp II at about 21,000. Jerry made a haul to Camp I, and then returned, solitary, to Advanced Base. He entered camp to find fifteen boxes, all closed but none sealed, seven personal duffels which had managed to get covered with tarps, and three team duffels just laying around, as if someone had walked out the door for a cup of tea intending to return. A quick inventory indicated that the climbers were shunning the group stuff—tents, fuel, food, ropes, etc. and packing their personal stuff. What would they do with down parkas when they had no food to eat or fuel to warm it with? Still, everyone was working hard and was tired; each of the climbers had hauled up to Camp I five times. And there had been a modicum of whining.

Jerry laughed to himself remembering the organizational fiasco climbing in the Pamirs with the Old Goat. None of the climbers on this trip, with the possible exception of Doug, had any idea of the time and energy that it had taken to get this far—and that it continued to take. Jerry sighed. His mind was working constantly at the calculations, the inventory of where the people were, where their equipment was, where the food and fuel were, how much they would need. He sighed again, deeper this time, trying to identify the nagging feeling in the pit of his stomach. Maybe it was just that the others had come to expect and take his preparedness for granted, and they failed to acknowledge, much less appreciate, the underpinnings that were really carrying them up the mountain. Which of them would think to thank Cyndi for the labor-intense months of planning?

Weary, Jerry dragged a duffel outside of the tent and sank into it like a bean bag chair. There was no one else in camp and the vast rubble mound of the mountain was intensely quiet. The stars almost seemed noisy in their glittering, if one could only decipher the Morse code of their communication. Then he heard the small tinkling of bells and looked out to see a group of monks walking in tennis shoes, over the Nangpa La, the pass between Nepal and Tibet, on their way to see the Dalai Lama in India. It was a still night and the snowy peaks reflected the bright half-moon onto the snow-covered pass, which rolled like a shining black ribbon up into a faint layer of clouds.

Jerry listened to the monks' bells fade into the distance. He woke early on September 19th and opened the card at sunrise.

From Boulder to Base-Camp, Cho Oyu
(To Jerry on the occasion of our 10th anniversary)

By now you will know
how many yaks it takes
to transport eight climbers
from Tingri Dzong to Base;
by now you will know
if our late-night calculations
have proved accurate
for food and fuel,
and if it was worth
the bureaucratic madness.

The Nangpa La (a pass between Tibet and Nepal).

Look down to where
the black, rutted,
glacial valleys curl
into the smooth twist
of the Nangpa La;
breathe an air which centuries
have not tarnished
with the concerns of a species
newly arrived, crazed
with the exercise of power
one over the other —
glutted on oxygen.

Poets and climbers,
we seek rarefied air;
only in the

troubled circumstance of
isolation does one truly breathe,
does one begin to know the limits
and liabilities
of oxygen
and altitude.

Each step up is a
step inward and
downward,
each view, a scar,
a carving of the soul by
the torpid
movement
of glacial ice,
each decision to move
higher, a risk
that makes untenable
the sedentary alternatives.

I knead words into lines
like the tsampa the
Tibetan people roll
into balls with their
fingers in their tea and
prepare for altitudes.

Beloved, shall we climb?

"How could you know I would be staring at the Nagpa La?" Jerry would ask later.

Later that day, joining the team above 20,000 feet, the trek finally began to feel like a mountain climb and it was with relief and a sense of nostalgic familiarity that Jerry laced the crampons to his boots in order to cope with the steep, windswept slope of perpetual snow. The date was September 20th and twenty days had elapsed since the team's arrival at Chinese Base. Some of the team were now occupying Camp II— at 21,000'. Next would be tackling the "ice wall"— a vertical face with virtually no exposed rock, just ice, for one hundred-twenty feet. This ice wall swept up through cliffs strung with great fractured fingers of ice. Here Edmund Hillary had turned back in his 1952 attempt of Cho Oyu. Tichy, in his 1954 climb, was the first to successfully negotiate the ice cliffs. Above that they would establish Camp III at 22,500', Camp IV at the rock bank around 25,500' and then hopefully push for the summit.

A Short History

Up in the death zone, success and failure
are as close to each other as storm and calm,
heat and cold.... And today I know that
the path between tomb and towering heights
is extremely narrow.

Reinhold Messner

Above 26,000 feet, in what they called the "Death Zone" the body cannot rehabilitate at a rate fast enough to regenerate. Prolonged exposure to altitude equals death. Cho Oyu is not Everest, but she is an 8000 meter peak. She was first spotted in 1921 during the British Mount Everest Reconnaissance when Lt. Col. C.K. Howard-Bury left Kyetrak (yes, the missing reference point on Jerry's climb), south of Tingri, for the Nangpa La and observed the peak from the west and northwest. In 1951, Eric Shipton, on another Mount Everest Reconnaissance, viewed the peak from the east and found "Not one chink in its icy armor," and suggested the only possible approach to be by the North Ridge or the North West face. On a climb led again by Shipton, Edmund Hillary and W. G. Lowe were turned back by the ice wall in 1952. Tichy, an Australian, with two others, S. Jachler and Pasang Dawa Lama, summitted in 1954, with Tichy, the leader, losing only substantial portions of his fingers.

A Swiss team, close behind Tichy and literally on the mountain at the same time, made its attempt only nine days after the Tichy triumph. Their repulsion from the mountain after reaching about 7,700 meters is well documented in White Fury by Lambert & Kogan.

In 1958, an Indian expedition under leader K.F. Bunshah, placed three (including Pasang Dawa Lama—the same Sherpa guide from the Tichy expedition) on the summit, but lost a member of their team, Major N.D. Jayal, aged 32, the first Director of the Mountaineering Institute at Darjeeling, from "pneumonia or heart failure" during the rapid decent. Now we would call this pulmonary edema.

I tell you this because it seems to us lowlanders that physical fitness is something within our grasp, something to be gained by training, and it is not always so. Altitude has its own take on the matter. One Everest summiteer, Oswald Olz, in attempting Cho Oyu in 1982, found himself incapacitated by pulmonary and then cerebral edema and had to be evacuated by helicopter. He had not been above 16,575 feet. But back to the history...

In 1959 an international women's expedition (four French, three British, three Nepalese, one Belgian and one Swiss) attempted the peak under leader C. Kogan. The summit team of three were isolated by bad weather and two Sherpa climbers attempted to reach them. One, Sherpa Chhowang, was swept away by avalanche, as was the entire summit team. This was the same Claude Kogan, famed lady climber, who had attempted the peak with Lambert in 1954 just behind Tichy's team.

In 1964, one Stammberger, leader of a German expedition, claims to have reached the summit alone. Sherpa Phu Dorje II claims they were together. I've encountered this offensive attitude before. Jerry invited me once to a slide show of a climber who shall remain unnamed wherein the climber claimed to have "soloed" the peak – an 8000 meter peak, but had a photo of herself on the summit. Porters and guides disappear in the Himalayan mists – it's the magic of the modern ego. We live in a selfish society, a society where all that matters is that you "bag the peak" whether or not your friends died to get you there. And there is no credit but the glory of one's own "success" viewed in isolation. For Stammberger and Dorje, the success was a dubious one—the photographs claimed to have been taken on top do not confirm, but belie the claim of victory for one or both. Two climbers on their team died. A second group decided to make a summit attempt and bivouacked at 7500 meters. Met there by the summit team, they renounced their attempt and descended to Camp 4, but fell ill and were unable to continue down. The four men waited two disastrous days before sending Phu Dorje down for fuel and provisions. Stammberger followed Dorje the next day, but himself collapsed at Base Camp. A 61 year old Sherpa, Dirdar Dawa Tensing, was the only person left on the mountain capable of helping, and he climbed to Camp 4 but was unable to bring down the dying climbers. By the time a rescue team arrived a week later, the two were dead.

In the coming years, the Chinese got serious about closing the Tibetan border. The next chronicled climb from the Chinese side was fifteen years later when, in 1979, a solo Iranian climber, Mischa Saleki, made an illegal entry into Tibet from Nepal, and reached the summit, only to be taken into custody by the Chinese upon his descent.

Attempts from the south, the Nepal side, were made. In 1978, Koblmüller and Furtner, from Austria, reached the summit, followed by Reinhold Messner, in 1983, technically avoiding the Tibetan prohibition by crossing above the Nangpa La to succeed on his fourth attempt.

There were two intervening attempts, with one German, Reinhard Karl, dead from head injuries suffered in an ice avalanche at 21,325 feet. Other climbs followed, some successful (such as the Vera Komarkova climb of 1984, which added controversy to our own), and some were not. Some were driven back by deep snows

(Messner's first attempt, 1982), fierce winds (Yugoslav expedition 1984)(Spanish climber and porter turned back by high winds on September 29, 1991), unanticipated and impassable geologic formations (Berry, 1984; Polish/Americans 1985), expired permits (Italians, 1983) and the injury (Spanish 1990) or death of climbers (Swiss, 1986). Some went on despite the death of a teammate (1992). Some used oxygen, some didn't. Some were women (On September 26th, 1991 Pole Wanda Rutkeiwicz climbed to the top. "It was the seventh 8000er for this remarkable Polish woman" writes Elizabeth Hawley). Some claimed to have forged new routes, but their testimony is difficult to attest to. Some admitted to having illegally entered Tibet to complete the climb. Others had proper Chinese permits. There are reports of frostbite in several of the climbs (Cho Oyu in winter, 1985)(Spanish, 1990).

Up Top

I do not know what unknown god sent the mysterious warning that reached my dulled and struggling consciousness; but from the depths of that stupefaction which high-altitude climbers know so well I heard the call and obeyed the danger-signal.

Raymond Lambert on his retreat from 900 feet
below the summit of Everest, 1952,
from "White Fury"

The team was split into two groups of four. The front team, Kent and Cathleen, Cleve and Karon, had put in Camp II and were to descend back down to Camp I for a day of rest. The second group, Jerry, Doug, Alannah and Dick, were to move from Camp I through II and take on the ice wall. Doug was the most experienced ice climber in the group.

On the evening of September 23, the two couples decided to ignore their leader's instruction and try the ice wall. Cleve and Kent set out to create a route by fixing a line of rope up the massive wall. Front-pointing with his crampons and with ice axes in either hand, the climber spiders his way up the ice, screwing in ice axes and attaching the rope with carabiners. The time consuming effort took longer due to the incessant cold, but by 9:00 p.m. they completed their task and rappelled off the top. Feeling accomplished, they proudly informed Jerry by radio of the progress.

Jerry was furious. This was the first sign of palpable dissention in the group. The actions of Cleve and Kent not only showed a lack of team consciousness, but were stupid and dangerous. Cleve had promised not to usurp leadership, and Kent, as co-leader, was equally culpable. There are always tensions in a climb, but what Jerry had first perceived as a nagging feeling of discomfort, he now recognized as a danger warning as he sensed his companion's raw ambition. Kent's motivation was increasingly to place Cathleen as the first American woman to summit Cho Oyu. Cleve and Karon apparently had the same agenda, and the result was that both couples had lost the sense of team participation. This is what Jerry, as leader, feared most, but perhaps his expectations of loyalty were misplaced. Maybe he was just grossly naïve, or romantic. Long gone were the days of his heroes—the Hillarys, the Herzogs, the men who thought and acted as a team. Perhaps the idea of team had disintegrated with Hillary's first step onto the summit of Everest. What schoolboy can tell you the names of the men who were slotted to and expected to summit on that expedition? Since then we have become a world of individuals—with little care for those who aid the process. As we said before, those Sherpas disappear in the Himalayan mists. Nevertheless, Jerry ordered the couples to stay put the next day and he, Doug, Dick, and Alannah prepared to move up for a total group meeting at Camp II.

On the way up Alannah was slow. What should have been a three-hour climb took her five and a half. She showed up two and a half-hours after the others at 5:30 p.m., shivering and weak. Jerry approached her and took her pack.

"My God, Alannah, what do you have in this pack?" It was twenty pounds heavier than what Jerry had been hauling, and it was all personal gear. He helped her into her tent, gave her some hot liquids, and said,

"You've got to move faster and lighter, Alannah. You are jeopardizing your own life and ours."

Alannah said nothing.

Later, at the group meeting, Jerry told the group he had talked to Alannah and addressed the problem. She responded emotionally.

"I've virtually been thrown off the team," she said, "I'm done."

Doug countered, "Hey, Alannah, no one has thrown you off the team…" but Alannah had reached her breaking point. So exhausted that she could not control her weeping, she bundled off to her tent adamant she was no longer a member of the team.

The next day was like those that had preceded it—cold and overcast, with a constant cold wind. At this altitude the body breaks down and does not regenerate itself. A cut in Jerry's leg from three days ago looked like a fresh wound.

Doug, Dick, and Jerry set out to look at the ice wall. The fixed line Kent and Cleve had set hung down 120 feet from the top of the wall. It would be hellish to move the equipment up the route. As they were about to start up, Jerry noticed a ramp-like feature to his right. There was a person standing there. She had appeared from literally nowhere. Jerry recognized her immediately as a Polish woman they had spoken to briefly in Kodari. Her name was Wanda. "Vanda" she pronounced it.

"Where did you come from?"

"There's a toonel," she said.

"A toonel?" Jerry queried. And they followed the snow ramp up, up through an ice fissure—a tunnel, which made a gradual ascent. They emerged to find themselves staring at a fifty-foot headwall. Two short fixed line pitches led to the basin above—a much more accessible grade than that roped by Kent and Cleve. Vanda's 'toonel' made the carry to Camp III a much easier enterprise.

Having established Camp III at 22,500, Jerry, Doug and Dick moved back to II. Alannah was preparing to set off uphill with Kent and Cathleen for a haul to Camp III. Rest had worked its magic, and she was a regenerated person. Jerry gave her an encouraging word, told the group about the 'toonel' and went to rest. He felt good. The team was back together. He'd done some real mountaineering—snow climbing, ice climbing, and rappel—and his muscles ached pleasantly.

But the success was short lived. Later that evening, Alannah struggled back into Camp II, half-dragged by Cathleen and Kent. She was hypothermic again. She didn't say anything; but, the next morning, packed her personal gear and headed down. Doug accompanied her part way. There were other climbers on the mountain below them, and there was no need to worry about her, but it was the Clint Eastwood thing to do. She would settle at Advanced Base where there were plenty of provisions.

With daylight, the others abandoned Camp II for III and began preparation for putting in a last camp, Camp IV, at 25,200 feet, where a vertical band of rock three to four hundred feet high stands exposed. South-facing, it gets enough sun to melt any snow that is tenacious enough to stick to its vertical face.

Jerry had instructed the two couples to move up, put in their tents, and sleep. The next day, as Jerry, Doug, and Dick moved from Camp III to IV, the couples would make their summit bid and move back down, through Camp IV to Camp III. Camp IV would then be available for the next three to stay the night and take their shot at the summit the next day.

The radio crackled at the scheduled contact time the evening of the 27th of September. Jerry answered.

"Kent here," came the voice through static. "Listen, we're at IV. Tents are up, but we're tired. We've taken a poll and everyone here feels they need a day before trying the summit. We're taking tomorrow off."

Jerry thought for a moment. "Okay," he finally capitulated, "But that means we'll all be at IV together; we'll have to bring tents. Tomorrow, make sure you clear us a spot for our tents and have water ready. If we all go for it the next day, we'll need all the strength we can come up with."

"Sure thing," said Kent.

And so, the next evening found seven at Camp IV. Dick and Jerry had been climbing all day, with heavy packs. When they arrived at Camp IV there were two tents placed, fully occupied, and no platform for a third, much less a fourth. Egotism had dictated over team.

Dick and Jerry swore under their breath and began the grueling task of chipping a platform out of the ice. Just existing at that altitude, in that kind of cold consumes more calories than a person can replace, and the work was draining the already exhausted climbers. One tent would have to do. Jerry asked the others how much water they had melted and was met with blank stares. The resting couples had been there all day and had apparently done nothing at all. Water had been a problem for a while. It is a tedious task to set up a stove and watch snow melt but Jerry knew dehydration is the fiercest of enemies at altitude; so, after cutting a platform and putting up the tent, he turned his attention to melting water.

Jerry thought about the situation. Although it was bloody cold, the weather had been stable. If the climbers were strong enough, tomorrow would be a good time for a shot at the summit. Personally, he could use a day of rest and rehabilitation. But the two couples were eager, rested, rehydrated, and competitive. The competition was becoming palpable. Jerry had ignored it thus far and would continue to do so. Several strong women had summitted this mountain including Vera Komarkova and Magda King. Their success did not make this eight thousand meter peak less challenging.

Doug joined them late, exhausted from escorting Alannah down and then retracing his steps before he even began the climb to Camp IV. He needed rest. Still, a brief team meeting was dominated by the restless and rehydrated, and it was decided to make a summit attempt with a 3:00 a.m. departure. Doug crowded into the Bibler tent with Jerry and Dick—an uncomfortable squeeze. The unexpected weight shift made it impossible to get the zipper to close completely. The position of the bodies forced Jerry's feet close to the tent door. Jerry fell into an uncomfortable sleep only to wake up every five to ten minutes gasping for air. He took a drug called Diamox to help, but it was an awful night.

At 3:00 a.m. it was still cold, but calm. There was nothing to be done to keep the team together. Dick, Doug and Jerry crawled out of their tent to find Kent and Cathleen already gone. Shortly thereafter Cleve and Karon took off.

Dick, Doug and Jerry decided to stay together, but not to rope. From Camp II upward they had been in roped teams but here the snow was deep and avalanches prevalent. It was safer to keep apart to avoid sending an avalanche down on one forced to follow behind by rope. Given the type and consistency of the snow, a personal arrest with an ice axe was more likely than a rope to save one's life in the event an avalanche was triggered.

Cleve increased his pace to catch up with Kent and Cathleen, leaving Karon behind. The movement was slow as it inevitably is at high altitude: one step, three breaths. The air was fiercely, fiercely cold. At this height, even the most trained and experienced climbers experience hypoxia. They talk of dragons, ghosts and voices that lead them. They speak of euphoria showing them the way and sustaining their bodies. For Jerry, the voices had something else to say. At the

Approaching the ice wall.

summit plateau (26,250), less than 800 vertical feet from the summit, our climber knew something was seriously wrong. He could not articulate it. He thought perhaps dehydration. There was no question he should have had more water. He'd always needed a lot of water. Perhaps just exhaustion. When drinking, smoking marijuana, driving cross-country, diving into deep water, or just being plain old tired, there is a time when the body delivers to the mind the simple message, "Turn back." One more gulp and toxic psychosis will take your consciousness and your body, one second more and the lungs will collapse. The danger place has been reached and the semi-conscious mind knows. Nothing of will power or personality can overcome the tenacious desire to survive and the blood knows survival is what is at issue. Climbers call it "hitting the wall." Tomorrow a different set of conditions may prevail and a different activity may be possible. Jerry thought that if he returned to Camp IV, he could sleep, rest, acclimatize, drink water, and try this thing again in a day or two. He turned around. Not long after that, Dick turned around. Doug turned around as well.

That's where the diary ends, with one final entry:

10-4-91 3:15 p.m. Friday Advanced Base:

It is painful to write. I have been gone a week. A lot has happened. The sound of Cyndi's voice on tape will have to get me down.

Grief and Grieving

Every soul carries the burden of fear.
Every heart is rent with the torment of loneliness.
Every mind has resources of despair beyond reckoning.

Stephen Tyman
from "A Fool's Phenomenology"

At last Jerry was working again. Each morning I drove him to work and helped him into the wheelchair. He was incredibly stubborn about letting anyone help him; and this particular February morning the chair slipped on the ice as he moved into the seat. I instinctively reached to break his fall and he growled at me, "I've got it, leave me alone." He resented me for being a participant in his need, or even a witness to it.

"You know," I said, sitting down on the curb and watching him heave himself back into the chair, "I've been so angry, so angry at those other climbers, your 'team' members, because I thought they didn't help you down that mountain and we know most of the damage came from walking out. They carried Tichy, that guy in 1954 with the frostbite in the pictures, they carried him out on a stretcher. Oh, I know you refuse to condemn them, you just say, 'we all have to live with what happened up there and we all know'; well, sometimes you are too god-damned stoic and you know what? You know what? I'm not sure it's their fault. You think you are so goddamned self-sufficient, that you don't ever need to ask." I hesitated, having blundered into my own cognizance, and then repeated with amazement, "You never asked."

"There was no one I could ask," he said laconically, wheeling himself away. And so he had walked down the mountain on his own.

In April we lost B.J. Hunnibear. As we'd moved into spring we'd watched him wane. Unable to get food to the stomach, the dog was literally starving to death. One morning the goofy old fellow was too weak to stand. The big brown eyes did not look up to greet mine.

Jerry was between surgeries. His feet had healed sufficiently to allow him to leave the wheelchair; but he was supposed to use crutches. I knelt beside the dog, but the animal did not raise its eyes to mine. The time had come, but I couldn't lift the dog. Jerry didn't complain, just put his big boots on over the bandages, stood up, leaned down to pick up the dog and carried him to the car. We didn't say anything to each other, but watched the veterinarian administer the euthenizing injection. Outside, we held each other in silence. It was the first time we'd embraced since he'd come home six months earlier. That night, Jerry reached to touch me, and I turned to him, grateful; for minutes we lay suspended in time, the lovers we used to be.

The next day Jerry put on the boots again. "Thing of beauty," he said as he got into his 1968 Chevy Impala ("Clarence"— Florence had been hit when parked on the street and her engine transplanted elsewhere. Jerry had bought this one from an estate sale, Clarence being its only former owner), jammed his crutches into the back, and drove off to work, alone. Most women rejoice at any evidence of sentimentality in a man, but we miss the clearest clues. It took me years to understand that when Jerry says, "Take a look at that thing of beauty," what he means is that 1968 was a year of transition, that his father let him drive the new Chevy; it had a 396 big block engine, and he still wrestles with mixed feelings about his father: anger for his leaving the family and yet respect for teaching his son there was no room in the world for prejudice and that big-bodied men must never, never use their physical strength to force their opinions on others. A 1968 Chevy Impala is not a car; it is a testimonial.

Jerry slid into the seat just like a teenager with first driving rights, revved the engine and left tire marks on the driveway in his hasty retreat. A sorrow overtook me. It seems there is no part of experience so repugnant that one will not miss it having once grown familiar. Having found Jerry's dependence upon me so distasteful at first, I had grown accustomed to it. I watched him with the trepidation of a mother seeing her sixteen year-old drive off solo for the first time. In ways he had acted like a teenager the last months, so sullen and withdrawn. Would he come home to me or use his new-gained freedom to escape from the pain of this place?

He had to come home. A visit to a new doctor indicated further surgeries would be necessary. Jerry would be homebound again. We scheduled the surgeries for late April. I was exhausted. Not knowing what else to do, I called my brother Stephen, a person who has had more than his share of care-giving nursing a wife with the most accelerated type of multiple sclerosis. Marilyn had been bed-ridden for years, and had recently lost the use of her arms.

"I don't mean to complain," I apologized, knowing his situation was so much worse than mine, "But I may not be strong enough… I don't know how to get through this."

"Get help," he said simply, rendering me the advice he had never been able to follow for himself. I took the advice.

Joan came into our lives with the brisk, cheerful, take-charge attitude one expects from a nurse. She was middle-aged and maternal. After less than a week of taking charge of Jerry's morning foot-care, she informed me that I was taking a weekend off. "You are exhausted," she informed me, "and you will help both yourself and Jerry if you get out of here."

So I signed up for a writer's conference in Missoula, Montana. It was entitled "In the Thoreau Tradition, a Conference on Nature and Culture: New Stories for a New West." The speakers were articulate and thought provoking and I was introduced to the stunningly good works of Marilyn Robinson, Warren Nelson, and the poems of Simon J. Ortiz. Listening to Simon Ortiz recite his own poetry from Before and After the Lightning was as moving as watching an electric cloud to cloud firestorm below the Maroon Bells in Colorado. But sitting in my hotel room that night I realized I had not come to be dazzled with the language of even the most articulate and gifted of writers, nor to hear about how the Western landscape is suffering. I had come to grieve.

So, the next day, I skipped the seminars and crossed the bridge from the hotel following the river until I found a path up into the hills defining the valley. It was my one chance to be alone, to experience the loss of B.J., the loss Jerry had suffered, to absorb the changes that had been wrought in my life.

I do not have adequate language for what occurred during that walk. There was sun on muscles rendered overtaut by months of anxiety, doctors, specialists, the work of lifting the wheelchair, the water for the footbaths; there was the monotony of rhythmical physical exertion, a relaxation of the vigilance of an overwrought mind, the tremendous relief from thinking that occurs when one simply engages in physical activity, the relief of not being engaged in verbalization; there was the mountain itself, fresh with spring wildflowers and new undergrowth, shaded by evergreens; there was the excitement and slight fear, the mystery, because I did not know my way.

And, in the shelter of rock and tree, there was a place where I let my grief overtake me. Huddled down in pine needles, I rocked myself and sobbed. Tears came, a wracking, gasping for breath— broken, a keening, a full expression of my sorrow, and finally a calming, a consolation.

That I found my consolation in the mountains did not surprise me. Wondering if Jerry would ever really find his consolation until he found himself once more in mountains, I returned to the conference, but the participants were not discussing mountains. They were discussing linguistics. It was at this conference that I became aware of the linguists' position that the encounter with nature is so colored by our language that humans are not capable of experiencing nature without reference to language or the language function. I didn't buy it. Later I would investigate the linguists in depth in order to analyze their position and mine more deeply, but on that day, I was convinced (and I remain convinced) that nature emits a healing charm on the soul that has nothing to do with language. While the conference attendees jawed on, I basked in the lingering solace gifted me by the Missoula mountains.

When I returned, Jerry was grinning over the letter he held in his hand:

Dear Sir,

It gave me immense joy to get your kind letter. It brought back a train of memories of the times we spent in the happy scene of Motherland (Tibet). How is your frostbite? I dream it every night, when will be your second expedition? Hope your bloody frostbite is cured. I received money from your friend Deepak in

Kathmandu and for this I owe thank you very much. I would like to tell you something about my journey. I started to leave Nepal dated on 27th April. I got a bus to Sildoling and changed to another bus to Delhi. I faced some problems when custom officer demand huge sum of money. I gave two hundred rupees to Nepali police and they allowed me to Indian border. And Indian police demanded three hundred and immigration officer demanded two hundred-fifty. And another police came after few hours journey. He took one hundred and fifty rupees. I really hated them. I stay at Delhi for three days and moved to Dharamsala which I think foreigners call Little Lhasa. Here is very good Tibetan doctor who can cure except for AIDS. I will look for some Tibetan lotion that apply on the bite. If you have the photos our village and Tingri itself, please do send me few. I really miss my parents and home. I miss my lovely yaks.

Takchoe.

"Feel like supporting a yak herder through dental college in India?" Jerry's voice broke at the word yak.

"Sure," I replied. "How many people have their own yak herder?"

But the next day, when I returned from work with a money order to send off to Takchoe, I knew something had gone wrong. Jerry wasn't grinning. I picked up a plate of untouched food by his chair, and carried it into the kitchen, noticing one gin bottle empty and another half gone. Walking back into the dining/living room, I saw a folded newspaper article lying on the table. The headline read 'Wanda Rutkiewicz disappears in summit attempt.'

"Wanda of 'Vanda's Toonel?'" I queried.

He nodded, "Kangchenjunga's North Face, nasty piece of rock."

"Ah, damn," I said, crossing to him. "We're lucky then."

My Missoula respite regenerated me, but I would need it. In May, with great ceremony, we had returned the wheelchair to the medical rental store. So I was surprised one night in July to hear Jerry talking on the phone to his mother: "Well, Mom, I'll be going in for some more surgery here in a few weeks," he said.

I poured a gin and tonic and wondered when he had intended to tell me. It wasn't the first time. Jerry had stopped communicating with me about his feet. I had begun to wander our marriage as I had wandered the woods, straining to know the weather coming in from the signs and sounds around me, overhearing him say things to other people, sometimes just casual acquaintances, and finding out we were scheduled for another surgery. Was it a punishment? At first I had attended every doctor's appointment but I had given that up once he could drive. Was it self-disdain, administered as easily to me as to himself?

"Surgery?" I ventured.

"Reconstruction," he said. "They've promised one foot at a time and no wheelchairs. The plastic surgeon and the orthopedic surgeon will work together. Can you imagine two gods in one room?" His voice betrayed not only his cynicism toward the doctors, but also fear.

The plastic surgeon promised that, using skin grafts, he could perform corrective surgery on both feet and have the wounds healed in two weeks. As opposed to the daily wound care for months and months commencing the day after surgery, he was sure this procedure would work. He took a different approach than other doctors and asked me not to change the bandages until he removed them ten days after surgery.

So, ten days later, we sat in the doctor's office. Jerry and I looked on with anticipation as the doctor unwrapped the bandages. We said

What more could we lose?

nothing. The doctor said nothing. We all knew, looking at the wounds, that the surgery had not been successful and we had another four months of wound care and wheelchairs ahead of us.

That August night, fully ten months after Jerry arrived home, was the darkest. I knelt before him, commencing once again the familiar unwrapping of the bandages, and there was a silence between us as vast as the glaciers of Denali. That night was the first time I wondered if he was seriously considering suicide. There seemed no end to our Sisyphean labor. There was nothing to say, nothing to do; and, it seemed, nothing to hope for. On the bright side, what more could we lose? Our home.

Reforest the Moon

The unendurable is the beginning of the curve of joy.

Djuna Barnes
From "Nightwood"

It was autumn and dark. It had not yet been a year since Jerry came home. A fingernail moon floated above the jutting red rocks to the West and there was the sound of creek—our creek, Bear Creek. Stepping out the door, I could hear the soothing sound of the water's course. In the summer it is enough to keep one up at night, listening to its rush; but even now, well after the turn of seasons, the slower-paced flow was audible. There was the chitter of raccoon kits. There was the sound of Jerry yelling, "It's those painkillers you take for those damn headaches of yours. They've got you depressed." The door slammed behind me.

I was fifteen minutes across town before I collected myself and turned on the headlights. Still, it was a moon poor night. By the time I steered the car up the mesa and onto the unlighted back-roads, I had increased the car's beam to high. In an even throb with the pistons, my dilated capillaries pulsed. The headaches had been frequent lately. And tonight we'd had a fight—over the land he wanted to buy.

"It is six acres," Jerry said.

"Six acres of nothing," I retorted.

He seemed adamant. He wouldn't let it go. He liked the house, he said. There wasn't a tree on the lot.

I loved our home. It was only a third of an acre but treed. Home to numerous squirrels and songbirds. We woke to the coo of a mourning dove, and slept to the sounds of the creek and its resident muskrats with their oily little faces, raccoons, geese, duck, even an occasional heron, an occasional raptor. We'd been lucky all those years having creek on two sides and a neighbor on only one.

Then, one morning not long after we lost B.J., we'd wakened to the sound of a bulldozer. The City of Boulder was laying a fourteen-foot concrete path and intended to move right along the creek behind our house. A sign was posted informing us, for the first time, of a public meeting on the city's intent to move forward.

Between surgeries, I rallied the neighborhood. Jerry had his healing to do. Also, he was working again and, after all, I was the lawyer. I investigated. What I found was a "City Master Plan" outlining the city's intent to build fourteen foot concrete paths down, around and through every creek in Boulder. It was my first encounter with City Hall. I researched the issues, spending evenings and weekends at the library reading on wetlands ordinances, on federal permitting requirements, learning about soil inundation, riffle ratios, about the myth of mitigation, about the creation and function of wetlands. I had never thought about what Bear Creek meant to me, but with the likelihood of loss came increasing definition, knowledge, appreciation. The birds, even the plants, took on names: bulrush, anemone, manna grass, smooth brome, blue vervain, reed canary grass…

The city called it the Tributaries Greenway Project. The impacts were tremendous. The construction was destroying the natural migration routes of the deer, the foxes, and other wildlife through the city. Sixty percent of Boulder's wildlife lived in the corridors. Ornithologists from the University said the impact of the construction had been devastating: many types of birds had been, would continue to be, driven out. The damage to the creek beds from the bulldozing was enormous. The city's own experts agreed.

One day in the library, reviewing the legal documents, I found that the city had divided the creeks up into many projects, four for Bear Creek alone. Why? To avoid federal permitting requirements? It must be illegal. It must. I talked to an environmental lawyer. Could Boulder be purposely avoiding federal requirements?

A small neighborhood group would never be able to fight the city, he told me.

"But this is Boulder, Colorado!" I said quietly.

He laughed, "where have you been hiding? Got color blind in the seventies and can only see green? Take a look at the city council. The agenda is "growth," my dear, and bicycles are big business. Why, Bicycle Magazine found Boulder to be in its top ten cities last year."

I stood before the Planning Department and reminded them that Boulder touted itself as being environmentally aware; that the city's study showed bike paths to be ninety-five percent recreational in their use, that they do not serve as transportation alternatives because they don't go anywhere, that people drive into town to use them, negatively impacting the valley's air quality, that polls showed air quality (not recreation) to be the number one concern of the citizens; and that saving natural resources and natural places for our children to know nature, to know quiet, is a higher good than providing twenty miles of concrete for rollerblading.

Then, after losing at two hearings and approaching the final plea to the City Council itself, while sifting through documents at the Municipal Building, I found an interdepartmental memo from the City to Planning. It changed the name of the project from the "Bikeways Construction Project" to the "Greenways Tributaries Project." The magic of language. And Bear Creek, my creek, was designated as the top priority project. The suggestion? First pave north and south of the residential area where some opposition may be anticipated.

So, it made no difference what the environmental impacts were even if I could prove them. It made no difference if the impacts were high as opposed to low. The City had made up its collective mind long before they held their first "public meeting." The process was a cynical one. And then I understood. The Planning Committee members had snickered at us in the hearings. They had laughed and twittered during the neighborhood presentations. The process was nothing but a venting session, and I had fallen for it lock, stock, and rollerblades.

We went to the final hearing in September, Jerry once again in his wheelchair after that August surgery, and I gave my speech one last time. We left angry, humiliated, silenced, evicted.

And so, just about a year after his return, we were looking for acreage. An escape. An out. And Jerry wanted this property, this six acres in the middle of farmland east of town. Pretty view of the Front Range but no trees, no wildlife, no life at all. When we first saw it, we called it the "moonscape," laughing; but then Jerry seemed to latch on to the idea of it – the idea of silence, the idea of isolation, of privacy. He wouldn't let it go. And we'd argued about it again.

I opened the car window and the shock of cold air made me reach for the car heater. Fields passed by, undeveloped. There were still some open spaces. I was probably in the backyard of Rocky Flats Nuclear Plant; I should be just about passing that now. Soon that would be the only open space.

Where was I going? I wasn't consciously going anywhere, but the roads were comfortably familiar and after a few minutes I knew why I had chosen south and west. It had once been the way home. Then, after I was married and the house on Bear Creek became home, it was the way to my mother's house. I had been embarrassed as a teenager when my mother stopped the car, taking out her shovels and spades to steal... *steal* seedling trees from the side of mountain roads for her bonsais, wrapping the tender roots in moss and garbage bags. It was embarrassing. She had moved years ago; now this was the way to nowhere, to some strange person's residence.

So, what to do? Was it strength of will I needed? Strength to say no to Jerry? Holding the steering wheel with my left, I fumbled to open the purse at my side with my right hand. The items were familiar by feel: lipstick, wallet, pen...pill bottle. The lid flipped off easy and the spilled ones would still be in the purse. I swallowed hard to get the pill down without water; but I had done it before.

I pulled the car over. As the tension turned to sobs, I pounded my hands against the steering wheel, rhythmically, to the pounding in my temples. Then I suddenly knew that I had not forgiven myself for losing the dog. My fault somehow. Not a good enough nurse. Somehow I, lawyer-woman, was supposed to save all living things: the wildlife, the creeks, Jerry...and I had saved nothing. Everything was lost: my marriage, my home, my dream of children. Barren, barren, barren. Everything was barren.

"Trees will grow," Jerry had said.

But it was too much. Too much to ask.

I gave up my grasp on the steering wheel and relaxed back, the painkiller finally calming, not the pain, but my cognizance of the pain. My hands felt warm. I thanked the drug and leaned back further. I drifted. I thought. In the last year, what had not changed? My marriage, my muscles. Months of carrying the wheelchair up the stairs, the heavy footbath from the bathroom to the front room to soak his injured, blackened, gangrenous feet. And then the snow removal, the yard work as the seasons changed, the work of two people devolved to one, and now the packing, the cleaning in anticipation of a move.

My fine blouses were tight around the biceps, the collar. Even my shape, my delicate wrists, my slender shoulders, had toughened, had been taken from me. Could I use the increased strength to make it through? I had the whole bottle of painkillers with me.

I slowed the car as farms turned to encroaching suburbs. There was development here too: a new shopping center, a liquor store, a giant sporting goods complex, and office buildings next to the reservoir.

The moonscape.

When I grew up there had been nothing but empty fields and I hated it. I had vowed never to live without real trees, trees big enough to give shade.

As I found the right side street, I breathed deeply and a calm deeper than that afforded by the painkiller took hold. The canopy of green was at least fifty feet high. The trunks were so big a person could not put their arms around them. I slowed the car to a creep until I came to the cul-de-sac where our family home had been, and then I parked. A woman about my own age walked through the lighted dining room. Out front were the trees I remembered as knee high: peach, mountain ash, piñon pine, all towering above the roofline. I thought then of my mother's hands: her cracked canvas gardening gloves; her finding meaning in the process of growing trees, planting trees—and when she couldn't do that, when she was stuck on a god forsaken prairie in the middle of winter, painting mountains covered in trees. I couldn't paint, but I could plant. I could reforest the whole of the goddamned moon.

"Is there water for irrigation?" I asked when I returned home.

"Yes," Jerry answered, "and a twenty thousand gallon cistern under the greenhouse."

"All right," I said.

Up top.

Jerry at Base at the end of the climb.

Going It Alone

There is no alternative to the one-man path.

Denise Levertov
from "Into the Interior"

Then came a time when the wheel chair was once again returned to the rental facility, followed by a time of crutches, and eventually a time when Jerry took on the responsibility of tending to his own wounds. Instead of joy, each stage of healing brought an increase in distance between us, nothing articulated, but palpable nonetheless. We were carried forward by the current of the river we'd stepped into, inadvertently or no, and there was an unspoken knowledge that we were moving toward something, some time when things would be different. Finally the time arrived. There was not a day certain, or a rising of the moon, or a chill in the air as with the change of seasons. There would always be problems with ulcers—wounds forming where the skin was simply not tough enough, but a time came when the healing was done. Jerry's capacity was what it would be. There would be prostheses built into special shoes to help him balance, and finally, there would come a time when, without ceremony, Jerry would

Jerry and I on our wedding day.

fit his prostheses into his old John Caulden hiking boots and head up Green Mountain. He went alone.

I attended to the reforesting of the moon, planting over four hundred seedlings, each drip-watered by over a mile of irrigation tubing fed by the twenty-gallon cistern under the greenhouse. In Colorado, if you don't water, nothing grows. I put my faith in a future some years away, nurtured by single droplets of water; but then the telephone rang.

"Which peak?" I heard him say and then pause. "When?" "How much?" And then words like "visa" and VE 25" and "white gas or kerosene?"—words that rent my complacency and replaced my faith with resigned sorrow. He was going to Nepal. He was going to climb. And he was going alone.

When he had climbed Rainer, Denali, Pik Korzchenevskoé, even Cho Oyu, I had not felt disconnected, abandoned, left out. I hadn't felt that way since the earliest days when he'd suggested I take the CMC course and I'd started climbing with him. Marriage since that time had been a state of mind, a journeying together despite physical distance, a collapse of conventional language defining separation and togetherness, so that, in truth, there had been no jealousy, no comparison even, no feeling of disparity. I had not thought of them as "his" climbs, but "our" adventures; but now, here in this place of no faith, of loneliness, of isolation, the ego bruised and the mind too active, my thoughts leapt back and began to rationalize, deconstruct and re-write my own history. There had been nothing to begin with. Our marriage had always and only been what so many others had accused it of being—an exercise in Jerry's narcissism, driven by and solely by, his desire, his mountains. He was a selfish, narcissistic bastard and I had been used. Losing him, just like all those unworthy friends, would be no loss.

The sacrifice had taken a lot from me, but I was strong. The place we had come to was loveless and it was time to walk away and concede defeat. I was not to be criticized. I had done my job. I had stayed until he was healed. He was healed, as healed as he would ever be, and we did not survive. That's all. Move on. Thanks to Takchoe, to Elizabeth Hawley, to Nepal, he had something to move toward. Did I?

The problem is in defining the ineffable—what has been lost—the thing that was there then that is not there now—the thing that allowed it to be a marriage, and not just a man, climbing those big peaks, the thing that was now absent as Jerry packed and planned this trip to Nepal, the thing that had been lost somehow, that was blocked, that had been suffocated by his unwillingness to accept me now that I had been forced to engage in what was to him an unforgivable trespass—knowing him in desperation and in need. The chasm between nurse and lover was too great.

I looked into the mirror, but I saw only the mask of the nurse—a determined jaw line, a pursed lip. If the game were one of chess, this would be stalemate. If a climb, then the moment when the weather whispers to the climber that the mountain has won, and he will not survive. No key to open the sealed box. No clue to offer exit from the maze. No rescue. Why couldn't Jerry ask the other climbers on Cho Oyu for help? Because if the climber accepts himself as less than perfect, as needy, he is flawed, flawed and not separate, not autonomous, not infallible. But surely the last two

A climber dresses up.

Everest (8848 meters) and Lhotse (8516 meters).

years had proved to him his fallibility? It was he who needed to look in a mirror, he who needed to accept his vulnerability. He who needed to ask. If only he could, only perhaps then….

But Jerry didn't ask. He went to Nepal. He climbed. And he journeyed back. During his absence, I had the above discussion with myself many and many and many a time. I was fully determined to ask Jerry for a divorce.

Reaching the Summit

Chant to me in your poems of our loss
and let the poem itself be the gain.

Richard Hugo
from "Letter to Hill from St. Ignatius"

"You can find your own way," I told him when he called from the airport.

There was a silence. I expected anger, but only heard a reserved, "I'll catch a shuttle."

He arrived with the huge duffels, but also with an awkward large flat package. Jerry handed it to me and said, "leave the duffels, let's go inside."

It was a beautiful photograph, fully four feet by three, already framed—a panorama of peaks.

"I thought it would look good in your office," he offered., "From the summit…"

"I don't want to know the name," I replied. "It is stunning, but…"

"But listen first," he said. I opened my mouth to continue my protest, but he added, "please."

A rare snowfall in the Khumbu.

I nodded.

"Nepal," he started, but his voice cracked. "Nepal is everything I remembered, everything I told you about the last time, the beauty of the mountains, the people. But it was different…. I had people around me: the other climbers, the porters, the guides, the villagers where we stayed, even some I knew from before, the Sherpa people. It is impossible to be alone trekking, dozens of expeditions use the same trails, herds of yaks, the Japanese teams traveling complete with table and chairs and chess sets. The walls of the guest houses are plywood. One is rarely physically alone, but….but," His voice broke again, "I was unbearably lonely. Everything was entirely wrong. The world was empty without you."

"I've never been on your climbs," I answered curtly.

"You've always been there," he said, "until now."

He was right. I nodded.

"I summitted alone. It was everything I'd dreamed—the Himalayan mountains, the silence so pervasive I could have been the only one alive in the universe. But despite my loneliness getting there, despite the absence of anyone else, for that one moment, I didn't feel in the least alone. This feeling of calm…" He laughed, "You are the goddamned poet. Listen to me trying to put it in words. Cyndi, it wasn't me who stood at that height. The definition of who I had been, was, was unclear. I could have stepped into the clouds without a care…."

I remembered my feeling that day (plucked from our ancient history) on Mt. Sneffels when I'd felt that way.

"…To define my feeling as confusion would be wrong because there was no sense of fear as when one is confused, no sense of being displaced. I was in the right place and it was the right time—all time was this place, this time."

He paused, "I'm sounding really stupid…"

"No."

"I tried to remember who you are, but your image kept slipping from me. I tried to put together an image from known facts: brown hair, brown eyes, but it wasn't you. Then I remembered the Liard River, but the wolf's eyes were clearer in my memory than your eyes, the sound of the river easier to recall than the sound of your voice. The words we said, I could remember them, but not how they sounded. Then the feeling of it revisited me, and it was the same feeling of well being, of continuity, with us and with the universe."

Jerry looked at me with some anxiety in his eyes, "Do you remember that evening on the Liard? Do you remember what you asked me?"

I hesitated, tried to steady the vertigo of my emotions and whispered, "Will you marry me?"

"Oh yes," he said, "I am so glad to finally be home."

High in the Khumbu district of Nepal sits a village where the yak herders call to each other in energetic tones while trying to shuffle their yaks into the stone-walled fields to glean the potatoes after the harvest. A monastery sits above the village at tree line, where only the tenacious survive. Small, wind-whipped pine trees like bonsai—the gnarled old men of the tree world—stand in little groups, sheltered from the wind. Prayer flags and stupas punctuate the landscape. Rocks with engraved mantras line the trail all the way to the monastery, evidencing hours, years, decades, even centuries of devotion.

The mist whipped in and out, veiling the high peaks in gossamer strands of light. In the dim light of evening, the low-lying foliage shone phosphorescent with autumnal golds, brown, yellows, and reds of a sumac-like plant. The forest green juniper shrubs and multi-lichen rocks added darker hues. The monastery itself is simple and old, a courtyard walled on one side by a stone wall, on another by a low, single-story building. The third houses a prayer wheel and the fourth a wooden structure on stilts, painted red, from which emanates the voices of children in choral recitation.

The children's chants can still be heard further up the trail. The trail narrows and seems to end, but it is a misperception—a rock protrudes, blocking the view. Jerry grabbed my hand to help me scramble around the impediment, and then we stood, backs against the granite wall, and found ourselves staring at a shimmering scrawl of gold on the horizon—the day's last light sparking golden off a high peak way down valley. Cho Oyu.

I thought I would hate this mountain that had caused us so much misery, and my stomach felt queasy. But it is impossible to hate a mountain. Cho Oyu was beautiful and we were at peace. Jerry stood behind me and wrapped his arms around, holding me tightly as we gazed on.

And then he said, "There's an orphanage in Kathmandu. I thought we might look in on our way back."

Such was a poet and shall be and is
—who'll solve the depths of horror to defend
a sunbeam's architecture with his life:
and carve immortal jungles of despair
to hold a mountain's heartbeat in his hand

e.e.cummings
from NO MAN, IF MEN ARE GODS

Acknowledgements

The author believes her use of quotes from other authors is a compliment to and "fair use" of the work of the other in the scholarly and artistic tradition; nevertheless, every effort was made to obtain permission except where the work is known to be in the public domain. The author wishes to acknowledge all such uses, and express her gratitude to those who have given their express permission. Additionally, a special thanks to the work and archives of Elizabeth Hawley as recorded in the American Alpine Journal.

Hamilton Books for lines from *A Fool's Phenomenology: Archetypes of Spiritual Evolution* by Stephen Tyman. Copyright 2006 by Hamilton Books.

Harper & Bros. for lines from *Moby Dick* by Hermann Melville. Copyright 1851; for lines from *Nostromo* by Joseph Conrad. Copyright 1904; for a line from "The Raven" by Edgar Allan Poe. Copyright 1845.

The Herbert Tichy Society and heirs for lines from *Cho Oyu* by Herbert Tichy, trans. by Basil Creighton, 1957. German Copyright 1955 Ullstein Verlag, Vienna. British Copyright 1957 by Methuen & Co, Ltd.

Hurst & Blackett Limited and Maurice Herzog for lines from *White Fury* by Raymond Lambert & Claude Kogan, trans. by Showell Styles. French Copyright 1955. British Copyright 1956 by Anchor Press, Ltd.

Jones, Marti for lyrics from "Follow You All Over the World" from the album *Unsophisticated Time*, A&M Records, 1984.

Knopf Publishing for lines from *Remembrance of Things Past* by Marcel Proust, trans. by C.K. Scott- Moncrieff. Copyright 1982.

Cloudcap Press for lines from *All Fourteen 8,000rs* by Reinhold Messner. Copyright 1999.

North Dakota Quarterly, for material from the essay "The Language of Mountains." Copyright 1998 by Cynthia T. Kennedy.

Penguin Classics for lines from *Thus Spoke Zarathustra*, Nietzsche, trans. by R.J. Hollingdale. Copyright 1961 and from *A Tramp Abroad* by Mark Twain. Copyright 1880.

Princeton University Press for lines from *The I-Ching or Book of Changes*, Richard Wilhelm Translation rendered into English by Cary F. Baynes. Copyright 1950 by The Bollingen Foundation.

Simon and Schuster for lines from *Journey to Ixtlan*. Copyright 1972 by Carlos Castaneda.

University of Chicago Press for lines from "The Eumenides" from Aeschylus I Oresteia, trans. by Richmond Lattimore. Copyright 1953 by The University of Chicago.

University of Missouri Press for lines "Tu Fu at Pike's Peak" from *All These Lands You Call One Country*. Copyright 1992 by Stephen Corey.

Alfred Publishing for a lyric from "Thirsty Boots" by Eric Anderson from "'Bout Changes & Things" Vanguard Records.

W.W. Norton & Company, Inc. for lines from "Letter to Hill from St. Ignatius" from *31 Letters and 13 Dreams* by Richard Hugo. Copyright 1977 by W.W. Norton & Company, Inc.

W.W. Norton & Company, Inc. for lines from "Sonnet 29" from *Sonnets to Orpheus* by Rainer Maria Rilke, translated by M.D. Herter Norton. Copyright 1942 by W.W. Norton & Company, Inc.

W.W. Norton & Company, Inc. for lines from "NO MAN, IF MEN ARE GODS" from *1 x 1 {One Times One)* by e.e.cummings. Copyright 1944.

About the Author
Cynthia T. Kennedy

Cynthia Kennedy is a practicing lawyer who lives in Lafayette, Colorado with her husband, Jerry, and three adopted Nepali children: Krishna, Sunita and Bishnu. Ms. Kennedy's creative work has appeared in a number of literary magazines and compilations, including: *Tribute to Orpheus: Prose & Poetry about Music or Musicians, Disturbing the Peace: an anthology, Eureka Literary Magazine, New Mexico Humanities Review, North Dakota Quarterly, Oregon East, Touched by Adoption, an anthology, and the William and Mary Review.* Ms. Kennedy's screenplay "Buddha Eyes" won the 2007 Columbine Award from Moondance Film Festival and Best Screenplay FAIF International Film Festival.